Partners in Literacy

DATE DUE

Partners in Literacy

SCHOOLS AND LIBRARIES BUILDING COMMUNITIES THROUGH TECHNOLOGY

Sondra Cuban and Larry Cuban

TEACHERS
COLLEGE
PRESS

Teachers College, Columbia University
New York and London

ALAEditions

American Library Association

Published simultaneously by Teachers College Press, 1234 Amsterdam Avenue, New York, NY 10027 and the American Library Association, 50 East Huron Street, Chicago, IL 60611

Library of Congress Cataloging-in-Publication Data

Cuban, Sondra.
   Partners in literacy : schools and libraries building communities through technology / Sondra Cuban and Larry Cuban.
        p.   cm.
   Includes bibliographical references and index.
   ISBN 978-0-8077-4795-7 (pbk : alk. paper)—ISBN 978-0-8077-4796-4 (cloth : alk. paper)
   1. Educational technology.   2. Libraries and schools.   3. Computers and literacy. I. Cuban, Larry.   II. Title.

   LB1028.3.C813 2007
   371.33—dc22

                                                                    2007004151

ISBN 978-0-8077-4795-7 (paper)
ISBN 978-0-8077-4796-4 (cloth)

Printed on acid-free paper
Manufactured in the United States of America

14   13   12   11   10   09   08   07   8   7   6   5   4   3   2   1

It takes a family:
With love to Barbara, Janice, and Ozias

Contents

Acknowledgments

We wish to thank the many teachers, librarians, and students who opened their doors, minds, and hearts to us so that we could attempt to piece together the puzzle of libraries, schools, and technologies for community building. It takes a community to write a book—we value their insightful contributions. Their names are many, some of whom chose to remain anonymous. Yet their stories and quotes are present in our book. Lastly, we acknowledge that without a strong relationship and good communication between a father and daughter, we could not have written this book. It was a natural next step for us to dialogue about similar problems we were wrestling with in different, but closely related, community-based institutions, and then roll up our sleeves to write about it. The experience of working together for over 2 years to write this book is a memory that will remain fixed in our minds and hearts forever.

Technology in Libraries and Schools in the Early 21st Century: Separated Partners

For nearly two centuries, libraries and schools have engaged in community-based education, focusing on literacy and dispensing information to the public. Yet they usually do it separately and are often unrecognized partners in this effort because, as technology reformers note, "schools, homes, and workplaces today function separately—connected always by geography and circumstance, but only infrequently by common purpose and collaborative action."[1] The following actual scenes display these invisible intersections of separate partners.[2]

SCENE ONE: 1999

Theresa, a woman of Mexican ancestry who owns a cleaning business, sits in a small chair in her Hawaiian granddaughter's school library opposite the girl's teachers. Together they carve out a diagnostic testing plan for the granddaughter's learning disabilities. For the past 2 years Theresa has been learning how to use computers in her public library's learning program. It has given her the confidence and the skills to interact with other professionals and to advocate for her family.

SCENE TWO: 2000

In Greensboro, North Carolina, Michael, an African American man in his early 40s who attended school intermittently as a child and is now a single father of two children (a 15-year-old and a child of 10), leaves them in the central room of a neighborhood branch library and goes to another room to study for the GED with other students and a teacher he respects. Next door is another room filled with computers, which are for his use and that of senior citizens, who come at night to use them. As a laborer, he built the library and even came there as a teenager. As an adult, he comes to this familiar environment to further his workplace literacy skills and obtain formal credentials to advance in his job.

SCENE THREE: 2001

Four adult English for Speakers of Other Languages (ESOL) students sit in small seats in the evening at a school in Redwood City, California, tapping away on laptop computers for the first time. The library and school have worked out facility space and a pilot ESOL laptop learning program. A computer consultant from a local company acquired these computers and through the local literacy program helps teach these adults how to use them for English-language learning. The students are parents of children who attend the local school, and their youngest children are being cared for in a room down the hall by staff of the library literacy program.

SCENE FOUR: 2005

In Seattle an undocumented Mexican domestic worker, Carmen, who previously attended a community-based program, goes to the public library right down the street from her to get materials for herself and her children. Although she is no longer studying English in a program, the library's resources bridge a gap in her education and add to the family's literacy practices after school is over.

These snapshots show the overlap of educational activities by community members in two neighboring public institutions. In countless other areas of the United States, libraries and schools work with technologies as separated partners. Yet without formal collaboration, schools and libraries don't know what the other is teaching and joint community resources remain invisible. Formal collaborations through technologies, however, may be difficult but worthwhile, as Louise Blalock, a Hartford (Connecticut) public librarian observed. The lesson this veteran librarian learned was to start small with a team of professionals who can work together. Through this effort, school materials were slowly added onto the public library database. She recalls:

> The benefit is on the school side and the school can see what the resources are. It is more efficient for them. It unifies us. It helps us see

ourselves as providing [for] the same population. It makes it better for students, too—more seamless, school to public library, it all works the same way. . . . The money for the school and the library and the police comes out of one pot. Working together makes sense. It's relationship building, and we are working with schools now.[3]

This collaboration has expanded to include coaching, peer training of school librarians, designated roles for libraries as homework centers, and work with at-risk teens who learn about video-streaming and creative uses for technology that they have little access to in schools. The most important aspect, however, was forging meaningful bonds in strengthening both individuals and a community.

In another collaboration across the country, the director of a library literacy program in Redwood City (California) has created mutually beneficial linkages with offshoot organizations that are loosely connected to the local schools. At one school, a parent receives tutoring and computer-assisted ESOL instruction in a trailer in the school's parking lot while her child is in an after-school program. The director of the library literacy program, Kathy Endaya, has nurtured connections with schools and their satellites over a number of years to create access to education for the many hundreds of people waiting to get into her program. She calls these wait-listed community members "the invisibles" because few public services exist for residents of this unincorporated neighborhood. Creating off-site programming near people's homes at local schools assists parents in receiving an education they might not otherwise get while obtaining library services at the same time.[4]

Through these library–school collaborations, the people who work in them share the immense task of educating community members, especially those who are socially marginalized. Yet these relationships are rarely seen. Because researchers and policymakers usually look only at one institution—in all of its variations—and the populations that inhabit it, it is difficult to see how people in communities move between institutions and learn in both. Cross-institutional comparisons, although few and far between, can illuminate a particular phenomenon—in this case, community-based education—through a common set of questions that are socially and historically grounded in time and space.[5] Some questions are: How can libraries and schools, working together, better educate both adults and children? At a time when both institutions have embraced new technologies, how can use of these technological innovations support community connections, make resources accessible, and nurture literacy? These questions are very different from asking what schools *or* libraries can do to better educate their populace.

We ask these questions because too often institutional collaborations, although hardly a panacea for deeper societal problems, have been ignored in the all-too-common censure of public schools. Technology, according to this prevailing viewpoint, pumps essential information into students—our future workers—who are positioned to fill holes in a knowledge-based economy hungry for skilled employees. With more front-loading of key knowledge and skills by teachers and librarians, students and adults—especially poor minorities and immigrants—will no longer be mismatched to the demands of an ever-changing economy. In these blueprints for success, technology at the local level, especially in libraries, is viewed as an on-ramp or gateway to expensive global resources, not necessarily as community knowledge. Thus, community renewal is neglected in favor of national and international economic competition. How technology can "reintegrate education into daily life" is not explored but is considered important because "the Internet is connecting homes, schools, businesses, libraries, museums[;] . . . draw[s] on significant experiences from students' everyday lives[;] . . . and will enable students to relate what is happening in the world outside."[6] We believe that bringing separated institutions committed to using electronic technologies into partnerships can revitalize fragmented communities.

Yet this partnership idea can easily lapse into opportunism. Reinvigorating educational institutions through technology promises to "reduce the educational disparities created by race, income, and region . . . [;] provide greater access to learning opportunities[;] and empower learners."[7] Vague declarations about access and social inclusion assume there are communities for people to join, ones with opportunities that are magically waiting to be utilized. All of these desirable outcomes—such as access to technology and reducing the digital divide—require altering policies and structures that currently block access and crimp freedom. What happens, for example, when some libraries and schools in upscale parts of a city have more resources than others in low-income neighborhoods? What happens when there are no Internet connections in homes or in poorly resourced libraries? What happens when libraries are saddled with filters that impede access to information? (About 40% of all libraries use filters.) What happens when real-life problems cannot be discussed in schools due to standardized curricula and testing limitations?

Access to technology and *digital divide* are both slippery and simplistic expressions.[8] They are also politically constructed.[9] Embedded in these phrases is the deficit-ridden assumption that poor and minority adults and children bring no virtues, no strengths, and no skills to libraries and schools. Yet there is no denying that a postindustrial economy places extraordinary demands on profit-seeking companies. Businesses "are faced with three choices: innovate, immigrate, or evaporate."[10] These pressures also create accumulated literacy demands in society because of the "insatiable need for innovation."[11] Those intense pressures translate into hiring workers who have the hard and soft skills that match employer demands. And that is where both public libraries and schools—promoters and guardians of literacy—enter the debate over community education.

Are there ways we can discuss access to technology or the digital divide without using deficit-oriented arguments? Can we recognize "the reality that many citizens do not get the necessary education at school and therefore must look at other institutions to provide that training and education"?[12] Some reformers have approached the equity issue by dividing it into gaining access, acquiring skills, and achieving desired economic and democratic outcomes.[13]

We, a former teacher and a former librarian, try to forge a pathway through the opportunistic and hyped-up debate about technology in schools and libraries (referring to its promise of delivering democracy, equality, and a better economy to the masses and the world writ large, as well as its role as sexy eye candy) to show the value of cross-institutional community bonds for learning with technology and of shared community-based education and resources. We focus on the historical and contemporary roles and functions of two community-based educational institutions—libraries and schools—and offer both theoretical and practical viewpoints on this topic.

Let's look closer at the lofty pledges of technology reform in schools and libraries. These promise a more informed citizenry, increased social capital, higher literacy rates and sophisticated life skills, well-educated families, and social integration. We do not fall into the trap of promoting any one outcome or promising that these collaborations can "fix" complex social problems that need a major redistribution of resources from all sectors and a communitarian vision. The value of uniting these institutions through technology is rooted in the historical relationship between libraries and schools.

In this sense, we build on their enduring identities as institutional partners in community-based education insofar as they are aligned with the public good: "If public institutions (schools, universities, libraries, museums) are to play a role in recapturing and extending democratic processes and potential, then the idea at the base of that role is the public sphere."[14] In this way, libraries and schools together can assume a stronger role in today's communities by providing diverse resources and dialogue and, in so doing, become the means for greater connection to the common good of educating the public, the very foundation of a vital democracy.

This view also means that institutional identities, relationships, and outcomes must be redefined as libraries and schools fill public policy roles, build their capacity through tighter partnerships, and map out a different route in their local communities. As one librarian argues, "Tapping into local networks and building partnerships is a great way to increase serendipity . . . each community is different and there is no formula which will work in all situations."[15]

The larger environment in which such changes have to occur differs from that in earlier periods. Current strong market pressures generate conflicts between historical goals and survival. Over the last few decades, critics of schools and libraries have asked why these institutions can't be more businesslike.

Choice, competition, and efficiency are at the very core of profit-seeking companies. Why shouldn't those principles be applied to government agencies? One might as well join Professor Higgins in asking, "Why can't a woman be more like a man?"[16] These economic pressures versus historical goals came into clear focus in the early 1980s during the Reagan administration when economic rationales started to dominate public discourse pressing schools and libraries to copy the language, structures, and practices that mark successful businesses, including the widespread adoption of new technologies to spur productivity. With these political changes, questions arise: Can libraries and schools accommodate these pressures for using technology and still perform their common mission of educating the public? Do school staff and librarians, using technologies, end up valuing the individual over the community and profit over public service? For answers to these questions, we now turn to concepts of community.

COMMUNITY-BASED EDUCATION AND TECHNOLOGY

At this point it would be useful to examine concepts that are casually thrown about, such as "community" and "community-based education." Then it would be important to discuss how they are conceptualized together, with regard to technology in libraries and schools.

Because the word *community* is a dicey term that has many interpretations and frames, we give it a sociocultural meaning as a group with shared values, interests, relationships, and interactions in particular locations and places in which membership may be valued as an end in and of itself.[17] In this way, community can have a strong emotional value when individuals feel a sense of connection and identity.[18] We extend this meaning further in defining a "good community" for the sake of conceptualizing working partnerships between schools and libraries. We agree with Michael Galbraith:

> A good community is people-oriented, controlled, and democratic in nature. It is concerned with the capacity of local people to confront their problems through concerted actions, directing themselves to the distribution of power, arranging for participation and commitment in community affairs, understanding how differences among people can be tolerated, and debating the extent of neighborhood control and conflict.[19]

Public institutions such as libraries, schools, and other educational organizations serve a common purpose in fostering and becoming guardians of a good community. In taking the concept of a "good community" seriously, we need to connect it to the common understanding of neighborhood as a place where people of a similar socioeconomic, ethnic, and racial background live.[20]

Yet neighborhoods do not always act like "good communities" in that people may seek support from outside of their immediate location; one study found that 80% of a White sample research population tended to seek out various services from outside of their neighborhoods.[21] Likewise, people may converse more with family overseas than with their neighbors or local library patrons. Consider a migrant worker who writes to his family in Mexico on his e-mail account at the local library. He sits next to a real estate broker who is checking her distance-education course discussion board during her lunch break. On his other side is a teenager who is looking up housing information for her parents. They are all talking to virtual community members, not one another. Their nonengagement with one another changes concepts of "community."

This is a reminder that neighborhood-centered communities need access via technology and support from local, state, and federal resources to sustain access. They also need a forum for civic engagement, whereby community members can interact and exchange information. The real estate broker might also have a family in Mexico that knows the migrant worker's family, and she might be able to help the teenager with her housing search.

So how can community-based education support and sustain individuals' sense of connection and identity while helping them face personal and neighborhood problems and still participate in solving those problems as community members, in a wildly mobile world? Any answer to this question begins with a brief history of community-based education.

Community-based education and *community education* are often interchangeable terms that focus on development and renewal of communities. The ideas come from the adult education field and from the community schools movement.[22]

The focus in adult education is on offering a wide variety of learning activities and programs that range from solving neighborhood problems, to becoming active citizens participating in the larger community, to pursuing lifelong learning.

Adult education consists of accredited educational institutions that offer diplomas or certifications. They also embrace what are typically called nonformal educational settings such as libraries, museums, and civic organizations.[23] These institutions tend to organize learning in more flexible environments with fewer governmental constraints on content. Popular education also falls within this category and may embed itself within community development initiatives. Informal learning, which is usually cast as learning that takes place outside of an institutional purpose, can occur in both formal and nonformal institutions, as with "open schools" for children or "open universities" for adults, or as self-directed learning in schools. With partnerships between formal and nonformal institutions, it would be possible to support continuous learning and persistence in education as all community members move through them during a lifetime. We can imagine community agencies "freely working together where school buildings, libraries, and museums are open more hours than they are closed." We can imagine "bustling communities within neighborhoods where individuals work, learn, and relax together."[24] Furthermore, we can imagine that community-based education buffers and helps disenfranchised groups find a "hammock of support" in neighborhoods.[25]

Collaboration between community-based institutions can be vital for breaking down societal barriers to learning, given the uneven distribution of resources in formal and nonformal organizations.[26] An example of this would be Community Partnerships for Adult Learning (C-PAL), which attempts to bridge various educational institutions to produce better access to and diverse learning opportunities. When adults can choose among public schools, community colleges, libraries, churches, businesses, unions, and other community organizations, they can find basic education and services in a variety of settings.[27]

Community technology centers, funded by the U.S. Department of Education, also respond to disenfranchised groups' needs through collaboration, using a wide range of partnerships and networking with different organizations. Although recently they have come under the No Child Left Behind Act and focus on academic enrichment, these centers are still geared toward breaking down barriers for different populations—from providing ESOL instruction, to promoting family literacy, to aiding in the acquisition of computer skills.[28] On a more local level, one library, for example, helped underresourced local nonprofit agencies develop websites. This project helped the library to reevaluate its goals in providing information and referral services to its patrons.[29] We consider such partnerships as interventions into complex community problems by bringing in different expertise and resources.[30]

Another stream of thinking about community education targets children and families and can be located in the community school movement, which includes full-service schools, integrated schools, or coordinated school-linked services. From this perspective, education is comprehensive and holistic, addressing marginalized children's multiple needs as well as those of their families. Families using school-based community centers receive medical, social, and employment services and contribute to both the school and community by providing social networks for new students and families. Families in the community can teach newcomers how to use health clinics, libraries, job centers, and computers; they can guide newcomers to participate in school governance and help build a sense of community.[31]

Technological linkages help considerably in guiding both new and old residents to and through these agencies. The focus, however, is not on technology as an end in and of itself but on accessing and using these services. These services include classroom instruction for both adults and children, student and family assistance, crisis help, support for transitions, home involvement in schooling and community outreach, and acquiring leadership and communication skills. These services allow school-based community centers to meet many, although not all, of the needs of children and families while reducing barriers to learning and fostering achievement.[32] None of this is easy to create and sustain. Much cross-training, organizational restructuring, and interdisciplinary collaboration is necessary, not to mention logistics—such as sharing facilities, paying staff, and dealing with complex financing structures in creating these services. Moreover, any approach should take into account the specific needs and unique traits of the community, including class and cultural differences. When technology networks are involved, these can create even more complex arrangements.[33]

There are numerous models of community-based schools or full-service schools, the most well-known ones being the Beacon Schools and CoZi, founded by James Comer. Other models include the settlement house model of the Children's Aid Society and various university-assisted models. Federal- and state-funded after-school models are also increasingly popular and probably comprise the most extensive use of technology.[34]

Key questions about using technology for community-based education remain unaddressed: Does technology change the definition of *community* or create new definitions? Does embedding technology into community education lead to a stronger sense of community? Some critics argue that "communication technologies are particularly destructive of this sense of belonging not to a community, but on a screen." They claim that in the Internet environment, "not only does no one know who you are, no one knows where you are."[35]

To counter these potentially negative outcomes, advocates recommend mapping community resources, creating databases on important community resources such as Cyberhood, a technology program that focuses on community renewal—through libraries, schools, universities, businesses, employment agencies, and health clinics. In this sense, libraries and schools, when working on interlinked projects, become dynamic responsive agencies to their communities, both as "community centers and destinations."[36] Critics and advocates have yet to fully answer these questions about technology's place in community-based education.

Other issues arise which need to be addressed as well. For example, a community education agenda for most schools and libraries may be difficult to achieve due to strong financial pressures to downsize or get co-opted by private companies. These pressures tend to create library-like and school-like services—from megabookstores to the latest productivity model that awards prizes for efficiencies achieved. In fact, libraries, once seen as having been revitalized with millions of dollars from the Gates Foundation in the 1990s, are now struggling to sustain these services due to budget cuts, lack of technical support, and the need to upgrade hardware and software.[37] One study found that only 14% of public libraries reported having sufficient terminals to meet patron needs. One would only need to go into most public libraries after 3:00 P.M. to see the truth of this finding. Since nearly half of American homes still do not yet have the Internet, trimming technology access from libraries and other community settings becomes a significant issue. Connectivity, with regard to both access and speed, is a major problem, especially among rural libraries. We do not expect these issues to change as libraries, working under post-9/11 pressures from the federal government, face new dilemmas in their ability to serve patrons as demands for new kinds of recordkeeping and restrictions on privacy generate alarm and extra work.[38]

Furthermore, librarians and teachers are often ignored in policy deliberations about community-based education, especially the support-intensive roles they play. As one observer noted, "when you listen to the visions of cyberspace painted by [Al] Gore, IBM, and many others you sometimes have the feeling of a place where a neutron bomb has gone off—of endless rows of cyberstacks where never a virtual footstep falls."[39] Such views of technology can backfire when professionals are turned into its servants and feel "deskilled" and replaceable: What happens when teachers and librarians alike become low-level technology technicians, and lifelong learning, as great as it sounds, is delivered to children and adults through private corporations whose primary purpose is securing a high return on investment for shareholders?

THE CENTRAL QUESTIONS

All of these issues, concerning community-based education and the uses of technology in the seemingly partner institutions of libraries and schools, can be fused into the central questions driving our book:

- To what extent do new technologies in libraries and schools transform their institutional core functions and purposes?
- Why do two ideologically and geographically close educational institutions—libraries and schools—appear to use technology in different ways, for different ends, and with different intensities?
- In what ways can these two institutions partner together for the common good—in order to foster among their students and patrons greater lifelong learning, build diverse educational opportunities in local communities, promote literacy development, and nurture community regeneration?

At first glance, observers would think that tax-supported public libraries and schools, both of which are especially sensitive to national political, social, and economic changes and are considered to be core learning institutions in U.S. communities, would adopt and use new technologies in a similar fashion. Yet the extents of adoption, implementation, and use in both institutions differ dramatically, particularly in instructing adults and children. We approach differences in the adoption and spread of new technologies in two community-based institutions by using a blend of diffusion-of-innovations theory (e.g., early adopters, laggards); institutional theory, which focuses on the linkage among an organization's purposes, structures, processes, history, and social environment; and learning theories.[40]

We then ground these ideas within a historical framework to understand these institutions' development and their links to social, economic, and political change. We believe a critical analysis that compares and contrasts technology usage across institutions is needed because much of the focus in the literature is on computer applications in separate institutional settings. Although libraries and schools are not totally comparable, we feel that they serve as useful case studies for inquiring into institutional change and stability, as well as societal relations, with regard to technology and the ways they can work together for the common good. In addition, we hope to shed light on the multidimensionality of schools and libraries in their adaptations of technology to move beyond simple stereotypes—that libraries mainly house computers, while schools use computers to educate.

As the above examples show, libraries and schools have far more potential than most policymakers have considered. In addition to the macroview, it is important to grasp a microview of technology use in both libraries and schools. For this reason, we use learning theories to account for the beliefs and attitudes learners have about computers and how those beliefs and attitudes affect learning. Finally, we explore the potential and barriers to creating community-based partnerships between schools and libraries.[41]

THE CENTRAL ARGUMENTS

We make a two-part argument. First, we argue that different rates of adoption, implementation, and use stem from the historical purposes of both institutions in their communities, organizational leadership, and the web of social forces and beliefs that give legitimacy to each institution in a community. Second, we argue that uniting a historical and structural analysis with learning theories can give agency to individuals in using technology strategies that work in particular institutional contexts. Since computers entered both institutions at about the same time, we investigate how new technologies were being used and the lessons that each institution can learn from the other. In both cases, computers have been essentially viewed as a public good. For libraries, technology provided both a rationale and a vehicle for giving greater information access and equity to the underserved in communities. It extended the educational outreach movement while expanding definitions of literacy to be more inclusive of new and different tools. In schools, on the other hand, computers for classroom instruction were foisted upon them. The rationale was to make teaching and learning more productive and engaging. But more importantly, it was to prepare young people, particularly those in urban districts, for work in an information-based economy. Yet learning through technologies, in both institutions, has not been fully addressed.

We draw from case studies on schools and libraries across the country and a larger literature on computer use in schools and libraries. We examined the literature on computer technology in libraries and specifically on library literacy programs—most of which are computer-based—between 1990 to the present. We used surveys of library literacy programs as well as data selected from library literacy computer-assisted programs in different areas of the country that planned and implemented technological interventions, especially computer lab improvements, aimed at increasing adult student persistence in literacy programs. The data on school and classroom findings come from recent case studies of school use and classroom research in many districts as well as reviews of recent teacher and administrator surveys of school use of computers.

SUMMARY OF CHAPTERS

Chapter 1 looks at the histories and purposes of schools and libraries from the 1800s to the present. We examine their common missions, especially as they originated within progressive ideologies and as they serve community stakeholders. What social forces impacted libraries and schools, affecting their missions and the introduction and expansion of technology? The first and most important issue is to explore perceptions of technology among various stakeholders of these institutions—the public, policymakers, the workers (teachers, staff, librarians), and students (including their families). These perceptions are related to trends and issues that affect technology's diffusion in institutions and how it is seen and treated, as, for example, digitization of information, pressures on schools from new accountability and standards regulations, funding, and expansion of after-school programs and year-round schools. Internal forces such as leadership, deployment of new resources, and organizational reform are also explored as key factors affecting the roles of schools and libraries.

Chapter 2 examines the similarities and differences between public libraries and schools with regard to their purposes and roles as well as to learning, literacy, and technology use through the lens of institutional theory. The chapter explores public and private funding of public libraries and schools as well as leadership and staffing issues, mentioned in Chapter 1 as key factors in technology development and diffusion.

Chapter 3 discusses teaching and learning with technology in public libraries, focusing on the influx of computers and their integration into public libraries throughout the 1990s and early 21st century, as well as student use of and learning on computers. We present case studies and surveys to illustrate concepts laid out in the chapter.

In Chapter 4, we concentrate on public schools' use of technology in teaching and learning. We examine previous uses of technologies (film, radio, and TV) to advance teaching and learning as well as early and current uses of computers to teach literacy.

Chapter 5 addresses why public libraries and schools have used technology differently for literacy and learning and the lessons to be learned from these different approaches. In doing so, this chapter illuminates the historical differences in mission, structural approaches to literacy, and public expectations for each institution and uses examples to explore the future of technology in each institution and within their communities.

CHAPTER 1

Social Forces Affecting Public Libraries and Schools

"Good schools need good public libraries," a recent slogan coined in an effort to stave off New York City budget cuts, could have been written nearly two centuries ago by reformers of the day. Public schools and tax-supported libraries, born and reared in 19th- and 20th-century social reform movements, shared similar missions of advancing literacy among children and adults. Today, recalling this common mission has become a survival mechanism during crisis periods since both librarians and teachers are educators, members of the helping professions.[1]

COMMON MISSIONS: GUARDIANS AND PROMOTERS OF LITERACY

Early 19th-century reformers in New England and the Midwest sought to end slavery, secure legal rights for women, and uplift citizens through free public schools and libraries. To read what school reformers and public library advocates said then about their institutions, one would think that they came from the same family. George Ticknor, for example, who served on the Boston school board in the 1820s and later was both a founder and member of the Boston Public Library in the 1850s, believed:

> A free public library . . . would be the crowning glory of our public schools. . . . It should come in at the end of our system of free instruction and be fitted to continue and increase the effects of that system by the self culture that comes from reading.[2]

Or consider Horace Mann, school reformer and Massachusetts Secretary of Education between 1837 and 1848, who called education "the great equalizer of the conditions of men—the balance wheel of the social machinery." In one of his reports to the Massachusetts Board of Education, Mann wrote that education of all youth "will save them from poverty and vice, and prepare them for the adequate performance of their social and civic duties." In another annual report, he spoke of the necessity for free public libraries: "With no books to read, the power of reading will be useless, and with bad books to read, the consequences will be as much worse than ignorance, as wisdom is better."[3]

Practitioners who were leaders in education and librarianship applauded the reformers. Melvil Dewey, for example, noted: "Our leading educators have come to recognize the library as sharing with the school the education of our people." Others echoed similar outlooks: "The school and the library," claimed librarian W. E. Foster, "are in an emphatic sense, complements of each other, two halves of one complete purpose."[4]

Through increasing literacy, schools and libraries sought to transfer the wisdom of the community to both the current and next generation. As a primary tool for educating children and adults, reading became the early and continuing mission of both tax-supported institutions. "Along with teachers," Theodore Roszak says, "librarians are the guardians of literacy; literacy is to librarianship what due process is to the practice of law and hygiene to the practice of medicine."[5]

Reformers advocated for literacy in both schools and libraries, but they also sought to protect morality. As Horace Mann put it: "Let good books be read, and the taste for reading bad ones will slough off from the minds of the young, like gangrened flesh from a healing wound." As guardians of both community literacy and morality, the common school and public library took root and spread in the decades before and after the Civil War.[6]

By the late 19th and early 20th centuries another generation of reformers, now called progressives, coped with the social and economic changes wrought by spreading industrialization and the migration of American farmers and European immigrants to the nation's cities. Urban slums, poverty, corrupt politicians, and monopolistic business practices topped the agenda of progressives eager to transform government and business practices that endangered public health, morality, democratic participation, and the spread of knowledge.[7]

Progressive reformers—mostly middle class and professional—worked to make corporate leaders responsible to the public, end bribery and patronage in state and city governments, protect the public from disease, and turn citizens, especially non-English-speaking immigrants, into Americans aware of how to improve their lives. Making institutions in both the marketplace and public arena more democratic and efficient became projects progressives pursued.

These reformers, committed to the belief that knowledge would emancipate the young and make adults into rational "informed citizens," also refined the original mission of both public libraries and schools. Librarians and school officials sought both organizational efficiencies and a broader view of their social role in communities. These ends were captured nicely in the slogan of the progressive-minded American Library Association (ALA): "The best reading for the largest number at the least cost." To lower costs, libraries sought efficient management of facilities, centralized systems of classification, and uniform subject headings—while at the same time carrying out self-improvement efforts for its many women patrons who flocked to libraries seeking fiction. At one point, library rules allowed people to check out more fiction only if they also checked out nonfiction. Fiction was thought to be damaging. As one library leader declared: "It emasculates and destroys the intelligent reading power. It is to that what an excessive use of tobacco, tea, coffee, or any other stimulant is to the system." Yet, paradoxically, libraries, by supplying the popular demand for fiction, increased their popularity.[8]

Librarians also offered services to immigrants, businesses, and children. New aids such as the introduction of the *Reader's Guide to Periodical Literature, Fiction Catalog, Children's Catalog,* and *Booklist*—an ALA magazine —helped librarians find the "best" reading for both the native-born and those who wanted to learn English and become American. Concerned about guarding American culture from foreign influences, librarians offered immigrants reading materials that would ease newcomers into becoming full-fledged Americans. Many of these materials were in English. But foreign collections were also used to attract immigrants to the library, and they brought a multiethnic influence that had been missing when patrons had been largely white and middle-class.[9]

Many urban libraries provided community services that schools could not. In 1911 in St. Louis, for example, during one week 27 organizations held meetings at the Crunden Branch Library for groups such as the "Debating Club of Industrial Workers," "Polish Self-Culture Club," "Committee for Social Service Among Colored People," and the "Women's Trade Union League."[10]

In public schools, progressives expanded the familiar mission of literacy and morality to include areas that parents, especially immigrant ones, had previously addressed at home but could no longer do while contending with 12-hour workdays, crowded housing, chronic health problems, and surviving on low wages in slums. Reformers made schools responsible for the physical, social, mental, psychological, and vocational needs of children—the whole child—as lunchrooms, playgrounds, medical clinics, vocational courses, and counselors became architectural, curricular, and staff fixtures in a far broader school mission than teaching the three Rs. Add also to that mission a cultural duty to turn newcomers into patriotic Americans.[11]

It is clear that 19th- and 20th-century reformers saw both public libraries and schools as being in the business of literacy and moral uplift, albeit one institution served adults who voluntarily entered libraries and the other instructed children who had to attend school. And that difference between catering to adults and compelling children to attend school is telling.

COMMON MISSIONS, DIFFERENT STRATEGIES

Schools

By the mid-20th century, state laws required all children between the ages of 5 or 6 to 16 or 17 to attend school, with penalties for parents who kept their sons and daughters at home. Most parents willingly sent their children to school; they believed that schooling would help their children become literate, know the difference between right and wrong, and succeed in life. School attendance climbed steadily through the early decades of the 20th century, particularly among high school students during the Great Depression. Compulsory school attendance and jumps in enrollment not only increased demands for more buildings and teachers but also influenced teaching and learning.

With the establishment and spread of the age-graded public school in mid-to-late 19th-century cities, the one-room schoolhouse where teachers had many students of different ages began its slow slide into obscurity. Teachers now worked in an eight-grade school with each teacher having his or her own classroom and students of one age group (e.g., 6-year-olds in the first grade, 10-year-olds in the fourth grade).

Class size in the late 19th-century urban elementary school ran between 50 and 70 students and only fell to below 40 after the Great Depression. While there was much talk about making teaching a profession and tailoring instruction to meet individual needs of different students, large class sizes required teachers to instruct whole groups most of the time in the late 19th century through the 1950s. In these self-contained classrooms, teachers covered the slice of the curriculum allocated to that grade and managed large numbers of students. At the end of each schoolyear, students were promoted or held back to repeat the grade.

Even as standards for becoming a teacher were raised by the mid-20th century to acquiring a college degree and taking professional courses, teaching in an age-graded school remained a matter of crowd control in covering prescribed content and skills while socializing individual students to the moral and work standards of the local community. If students showed up daily, listened to the teacher, did their assignments, and performed well on the tests, they were promoted to the next grade. If they didn't attend or if they came to school and failed to abide by the teacher's directions and pass tests, they repeated grades until they got tired of doing so and dropped out. Measures of student and school success then and now were attendance rates, tests passed, promotions/retention, and graduation from high school. But these indicators were not tied to literacy levels.[12] Literacy was defined in the late 19th and early 20th centuries as being able to read, write, and do simple arithmetic in everyday tasks—functional literacy—upon completion of elementary school. Literacy was not defined by passing tests given in school.

If compulsory attendance pressed school districts to build more age-graded buildings and hire better-trained teachers, those same pressures also shaped pedagogy and, most important, inserted into the school equation the need to motivate students.[13]

That enthusiasm to learn varied greatly among young children and youth required to march grade by grade through school should surprise few readers. Some students needed little incentive to read books, listen to teachers, do homework, and achieve. Spurred by curiosity and a strong desire to learn, they looked forward to going into first grade as they did years later to taking high school physics. Others needed a nudge from parents who saw education as an escalator carrying their daughters and sons to a better economic situation than the one they were mired in. Parents pushed their children to sit year after year in classrooms learning content that had little bearing on their daily life. For these students, occasional gifted teachers sparked lifelong interests in Shakespeare, math puzzles, and scientific questions. But for most students, after the novelty of kindergarten faded, when parental pressure lagged, and as fear of low marks failed to spur interest in school, teachers had to find daily ways of persuading elementary and especially secondary students to listen in class, do their work, abide by the rules, and learn.

Over the decades, motivating children and youth to learn has taken many paths outside and inside the nation's public schools. Many families gave (and still do) sons and daughters money, gifts, and extra privileges for achieving high marks. Public schools, especially in big cities where attendance and academic performance lag, have offered (and still do) incentives such as prizes and cash to attend school and do well in their studies. Failing a grade and repeating the year drove some students to perform school tasks. These external rewards and penalties have spurred some students to learn, but not all.

Libraries

By the early 1900s, children were permitted to enter and take out books. As one New Yorker remembered her library branch in the 1920s:

> The library made me my own absolutely special and private person with a card that belonged to no one but me, offered hundreds of books, all mine and no test on them, a brighter more generous school than P.S. 59.[14]

Most of the time, public librarians guided individual patrons to the collection. "I cannot have information I know would be of interest to someone," a veteran librarian said, "and not share it." More often than not, teaching is one to one and learning is voluntary. Librarians (and those tutors, either hired or voluntary, housed in the building) seldom worried about motivating someone to learn; adults and children came with queries and topics to explore. Like schools, public libraries, past and present, do educate—both are community-based institutions—but differ in how they teach and how students and patrons learn.[15]

Historically, librarians have carried out their mission of democratizing literacy and providing moral uplift through building collections of the "best" books. Like teachers seeking to become professionals in the decades bracketing the turn of the 20th century, librarians wanted to be more than caretakers of collections; they sought to become a profession with a unique expertise and authority as they discharged their mission. And in achieving that mission while becoming a profession, tensions among conflicting values inexorably arose. Reconciling the need, for example, to provide the best literature with the need to serve many in the community who wanted popular (less than the "best") materials, while also attracting a sufficient number of adults to justify a tax-supported institution and guarding children's morality and community standards—all of these competing values caused much handwringing among librarians

Aware that they had to negotiate these tensions, librarians spoke out frequently in the early decades of the 20th century against dime novels and the racy *National Police Gazette* being placed on their shelves. At the same time, librarians accepted the inevitable strain of these competing values by purchasing *Popular Mechanics*, Book of the Month Club selections, and Marcel Proust while keeping Rabelais's books and sex manuals under lock and key. As "apostles of culture" yet eager to become professionals who educate adults and children, librarians found that their impulse to regulate reading matter warred with their impulse to get members of the community to enter libraries and learn.[16] Librarians had to keep taking on new purposes (e.g., recreation), embedding them into the mission, in order to survive—making the mission both easier and harder to justify, a century later, by historians:

> It will have to be as an educational rather than a recreational institution. The public library collection will have to reflect the long-term needs of the society it supports rather than the transitory desires of that small portion of the public that reads for amusement. This will fit with the increasing needs of an information-based society.[17]

Because libraries are tax-supported institutions responsible to elected officials and voters, determining how well they were achieving their conflict-filled mission required tangible measures of success. Then and now, "visits" by adults and children to libraries and circulation figures dominate discussions of how well public libraries serve their mission.[18] Even as circulation and visit statistics rose and fell, librarians felt the pressure for increasing the numbers. One among many professionals spoke out in the early 1950s "against the hypnotic influence of circulation figures and the tides of facile and superficial reading."[19]

How many adults and children did use libraries in the 20th century and who were they? In a post–World War II study, Bernard Berelson, dean of the Graduate Library School at the University of Chicago, found that less than 20% of adults and 50% of children and youth used the public library at least once a year. To the dean, the library's mission of serving everyone was a myth. Those adults who borrowed books and materials, according to his findings, were a small fraction of the population and were largely middle-class and educated patrons. Indelicately, Berelson concluded:

> Thus, just as many lawyers will tell you that their objective is to see justice done, whereas they are actually out to win cases, so many librarians will tell that education is their objective, when they are busy trying to increase circulation.[20]

Although libraries have changed a great deal since the mid-20th century, data collection continued to focus on circulation figures: How many people have library cards, visit, take out books and nonprint materials, and use computers and other resources? Much less research existed about what people learned and gained from their experiences of using the library. Enter the 1960s.

SOCIAL FORCES THAT INTENSIFIED MISSIONS AND STRATEGIES IN THE LATE 20TH CENTURY

The gap between the professed mission of serving everyone while guarding morality and the reality of serving an educated elite pushed librarians to expand and diversify their services, particularly after the 1960s. The civil rights movement, in concert with profound demographic and economic changes in the closing decades of the 20th century and early 21st century, washed across both public libraries and schools, revamping traditional expectations and beliefs about community-serving roles that schools and libraries perform. How did these viewpoints emerge?

In the years following World War II, Americans flocked into newly built suburbs across the nation. These suburbs drained cities of their largely White population at the same time that minorities and immigrants replaced those leaving. Those demographic changes coincided with the civil rights movement, which began in the South by challenging racial segregation in schools, transportation, hotels, parks, and other public accommodations. Building on *Brown v. Board of Education* (1954), Black-led sit-ins, demonstrations, and boycotts initially challenged Jim Crow practices in the South but soon spread through the rest of the nation by the mid-1960s.

With President John F. Kennedy gingerly embracing civil rights goals after the dramatic March on Washington in 1963 and, after his assassination, his successor Lyndon B. Johnson identifying with those goals, the civil rights movement became national. Its initial goals of dismantling segregated facilities shifted to eliminating poverty, improving urban schools, and reducing high unemployment and slum housing in ghettos. The shame of poverty in a country overflowing with affluence angered many seeking social justice. The divide between the poor and affluent grew wider in each decade.

The civil rights movement also intersected with mounting antiwar protests as the rapidly growing military involvement of the United States in South Vietnam sought, under Presidents Kennedy and Johnson, to forestall, according to the nation's leaders, the takeover of that country by communist North Vietnam. Johnson's efforts to build a Great Society and end poverty in the nation foundered in the escalating number of U.S. soldiers' deaths and billions of dollars spent to finance both the war and the Great Society programs.[21]

By the early 1970s, the civil rights movement, successful in ending Jim Crow laws in the South, was ripped apart in coping with internal disagreements among leaders and urban riots between 1965 and 1968, a year that saw the assassination of the civil rights leader Martin Luther King Jr.—who argued that the antiwar and civil rights movements were indistinguishable— and Robert Kennedy, an antiwar candidate for president. Although some laws were abolished, in practice, systematic discrimination in bank loans, farm subsidies, and admission to higher education continued across public and private institutions.

The antiwar struggle had already driven Johnson from the White House and installed Richard M. Nixon, who promised to end the war in Southeast Asia. Within a few years, a domestic political scandal triggered by White House operatives who broke into Democratic Party offices in the Watergate complex in 1972 to ensure the reelection of Nixon led to his resignation as president 2 years later. The scandal and resignation fueled profound cynicism among the general public and distrust of government.[22]

The political, social, and economic consequences of these events rippled through American society and culture. The media amplified the effects of racial polarization, urban riots, and the spread of drugs and sexual experimentation among the young and mostly White middle class. The erosion of trust in government, the decline of confidence in the nation's leaders, and the weakening of traditional sources of moral authority in schools, higher education, the military, places of worship, and the home caused many Americans to worry that things were out of control—the traditional center would not hold, as one historian put it.[23]

Politicians and voters shouted at one another. What worsened an already pessimistic mood among many Americans about a culture in which traditional rules and customs were being upended was steadily rising inflation in the early 1970s (the continuing costs of Vietnam and an Arab oil boycott had driven prices up), tied to an unexpected spike in unemployment and a decline in the U.S. share in global automobile and electronic markets.[24]

By the 1980s, fears of losing competitively to Japan, Germany, and other nations drove business and civic elites to investigate why the United States was economically less competitive and coping unsuccessfully with the fall-out of the Vietnam War, Watergate, and cultural changes that divided the nation domestically and weakened it internationally. The answer slowly emerged as blue-ribbon commission after commission certified that the problem was the failure of public schools to educate the next generation for a rapidly changing postindustrial society.[25] Not only schools, but also all public services, were scrutinized, as they were seen as part of this problem.

Schools

As a result of demographic and political changes after World War II, social movements to correct injustices, and a growing economic divide between the haves and have-nots, a three-tiered system of schooling had evolved.

Civil rights education activists exposed for the first time this multilayered system of schooling. A top tier of schools, about one in ten, exceeded the academic standards and scores in the top range on standardized achievement tests administered by districts and states. In affluent suburbs—or highly selective urban schools—mostly White students, with a scattering of minorities, had at their fingertips an array of mental health professionals, doctors, lawyers, and counselors to solve any problems that might arise. They went to schools resembling college campuses. Another four to five of those ten schools—the second tier—either already met or came close to state standards and scored in the middle to upper ranges on standardized tests. In first-ring suburbs and small cities, these schools retained parent support and had adequate resources to make up deficits when families came up short in helping their sons and daughters. The rest, the schools in the bottom tier, performed well below state standards and inhabited the lower quartile of distribution in academic achievement.

Most of these third-tier schools were in big cities and rural areas with high concentrations of poor and minority families. As part of Great Society initiatives, the Elementary and Secondary Education Act of 1965 (ESEA) thrust the federal government squarely into the role of improving schools for children from poor families. The law gave states funds for local school boards to improve those low-performing schools serving poor students. They were important supports. But they did not fully compensate for intractable poverty, institutionalized racism, and, most importantly, the tax base that schools primarily relied on for improvements.

Within a decade, however, national and state officials as well as business leaders, worried about economic competition in global markets and the poor performance of U.S. students on international tests, framed the country's social and economic problems as the failure of all schools—not just those in the bottom tier. They pushed states and the federal government to take a much larger role in school improvement. What assumptions drove these business elites and state and federal leaders to focus on public schools as both the problem and solution to the nation's economic and social ills?

Federal, state, and district school reform policies over the past quarter-century are chiefly rooted in the following assumptions:

1. According to national and international tests, U.S. students had insufficient knowledge and skills, and this mediocre performance imperiled the country's global economic performance. Low scores on these tests, in particular, signaled to policymakers that previously acceptable literacy standards for an industrial society were insufficient for entry-level workers in a postindustrial society and that children would grow up to be inadequate parents, workers, and citizens.
2. These student deficits occurred because school officials and practitioners resisted competition, opposed being held accountable for student outcomes, lacked managerial expertise, and tolerated low academic standards.
3. Therefore, more authority over local schools had to shift from local to state and federal agencies, even private companies, to develop uniform academic standards, require more tests, hold students and teachers accountable while promoting parental choice and innovation through school competition, especially for those failing to meet the predetermined standards
4. With uniform academic standards, more tests, and accountability, students would be motivated to perform better than they had on tests, graduate ready to enter college or the job market, and leave school with a clear set of hard and soft skills needed to thrive in the workplace and community.[26]

What policymakers forgot was the disparity in resources across communities, the responsibilities of workplaces (to create good jobs and provide training), and the downsizing of public services. Industry and business reformers were blind to these pervasive factors. What's more, teachers, who knew children's everyday needs, were not involved in these decisions.

U.S. presidents, state governors, legislator–business roundtables, CEOs and elected officials pressed for more state and federal action to improve the nation's schools. President George H. W. Bush gathered all of the state governors in 1989 for an unprecedented summit to set six national goals for public schools to reach by 2000. Some states—such as New York, Texas, California, and Florida—assumed major funding responsibility for their districts and developed curricular, instructional, testing, and accountability policies for local school boards. Federal and state officials and corporate donors pushed educators to wire their schools and buy the latest information and communication technologies so that students would be prepared for an information-based economy.

These moves toward centralized control ironically occurred during the years when the former Soviet Union and its satellites in Eastern Europe dismantled government-dominated command economies and turned to private ownership, market competition, and meeting consumer demand for a variety of products. Privatization hit American schools, too. Public charter schools, the takeover of failing schools by for-profit organizations, and voucher programs sending public school children to private and religious schools altered the face of many urban districts, while testing and accountability regulations affected each of the three tiers of schooling. The victory of market capitalism over state-run economies gave a boost to those seeing schools as public monopolies that had grown bureaucratically rigid, uninnovative, and unaccountable.

By the late 1990s, most states and districts had adopted policies to make public schools more responsive to employer demands for skilled workers, better management, and accountability—part of an audit culture that would assure success and progress. School board members and superintendents now spoke of satisfying customers, benchmarking progress, securing quality control, and holding students and teachers accountable for academic performance. Parents supported the quest for higher standards, more testing, accountability, and choice of schools to which to send their children.[27]

These arguments about linking economic reforms to higher literacy and social justice[28] culminated in the federal No Child Left Behind Act (NCLB), a reauthorization of the original ESEA law that President George W. Bush signed in 2002. President Bush, former Texas governor and advocate of testing and accountability, said, in characteristically blunt language, "Good jobs begin with good schools." To the president and his supporters in the corporate community, NCLB was a jobs bill.[29]

The law requires testing of all children in grades 3 through 8 in reading and math and, beginning in 2007, science. NCLB expects every student's test scores—displayed publicly by categories such as minority membership, English language learners, and special-needs subgroups—to display "adequate yearly progress" (AYP). By 2014, all students would be expected to be pro-

ficient in reading, math, and other subjects, thereby wiping out the historical achievement gap between White and minority students. Furthermore,
NCLB demands that a qualified teacher be placed in every classroom in the
country and mandates that schools failing to raise test scores for 2 years in
a row provide tutoring and other special help to low-performing children
and give parents the choice to transfer them better schools. If no improvement occurs in subsequent years, the school is taken over by district and state
authorities.[30]

The federal law pushed states further in the direction that many had
already moved as regards higher academic standards, more testing, and accountability. These federal and state laws assumed that skill-based education and higher levels of functional literacy were the high-octane fuel for
boosting poorly performing schools, making the economy stronger, and producing a more just society. What about public libraries?

Libraries

Entering one of the 16,000 public libraries in the United States today is voluntary, not compulsory. When individual choice determines whether community
members use an institution's services—as is the case with banks, supermarkets, faith-based organizations, and private schools—attracting potential
users becomes an imperative. Instead of paying to borrow books from an
early 20th-century private library or buying a book, individual Americans
could go to tax-funded public libraries and take out books for free. All a
person has to do is register at a library and receive a card in order to sit and
read, take out books, or use the computers. No charge. People come to libraries as individuals and families, to learn something in a public setting
surrounded by other members of the community. To achieve the mission of
promoting and guarding literacy and serving the community, how did libraries
educate adults and children?[31]

Adults usually know what they want in the library and get the materials to read, view, and learn themselves. Others who are uncertain go to the
reference librarians—including specialists who serve children—for help. As
one librarian put it, "I love helping people for free. I like the 'Aha' moment
when I'm explaining something and I see a patron understand it and get happy
all at once." And, yes, librarians, past and present, teach classes that range
from tracking family trees online to helping Vietnamese speakers use the
Internet. All who sign up come willingly. Yet seldom do librarians call adult
patrons "students" except in those occasional classes offered by the library.[32]

Public libraries in the past half-century, as voluntary institutions committed to educating individual adults and children, have had to adjust to the
massive demographic changes in cities and suburbs by accommodating their
traditional mission of giving patrons free access to information. In the South

and elsewhere, as racial barriers fell, Black patrons could enter the front door of libraries and have full access to collections. In the suburbs, public libraries, like schools, flourished, offering new and traditional services to existing patrons within their freshly minted communities. Still, like schools, some libraries were better resourced than others.

In cities, libraries still pursued their community role of advancing literacy, providing free access to information, and guarding morality in becoming responsive to immigrants, low-income minorities, and other groups seeking services. The growth of Information and Referral services, for example, testifies to the shift, not in mission, but in strategies tailored to largely minority and poor patrons. In 1971, the Detroit Public Library established "The Information Place," where librarians had developed card files listing the hours, addresses, and telephone numbers of local and county social service, employment, legal, medical, and housing organizations. With improved electronic data processing, these were converted to easily accessible files for patrons to use.[33]

With immigrants migrating from Mexico, Central America, and Asia to U.S. cities, beginning in the 1970s and showing no inclination to slow down in the 1990s, libraries resumed their community role of helping newcomer adults, youth, and children gain access to information. Federal monies helped libraries serve immigrants in various outreach programs, and these continue today as communities demand more and different resources.

At the Des Plaines (Illinois) Public Library, for example, Hector Marino told his computer class in Spanish to use *el raton* (the mouse) to begin *correo electronico* (e-mail) as he walked around the room checking on his adult students. At the New York Public Library's West Farms branch in the Bronx, 16-year-old Melquan Jones, a junior at Samuel Gompers High School, was at a computer writing down information on the history of the printing press for a class report. He would get up occasionally to look through a few books nearby, but making it clear to a reporter that "I come here mostly for the computers." City and county libraries that served low-income and minority patrons again revived their earlier roles as educational and cultural institutions providing a quiet spot away from the street to read, a source of job information, a place to identify a medical clinic, and, surely, a safe place for children to do homework.[34]

And, yes, libraries, like schools, have had to adjust to changing economic conditions—in particular, the rise and fall of federal and state funding and unceasing pressure to cut costs. The constant search for efficiencies, the explosion of scientific data, and adjustment of the historic mission of libraries to the changed circumstances of post–World War II America pressed library leaders to alter training and operations. Beginning in the mid-1990s, most graduate schools preparing librarians changed their titles from "library school" to "school of library and information sciences." Libraries adopted automated data processing, ending decades of patrons using wooden drawers holding card catalogs. Machine-readable catalogs (MARCs) were state of the art in the late 1960s. Professional librarians embraced automation and newly emerging technologies as the future course of public libraries.

Even with the shift from manual use of card catalogs to quick clicks of terminal keys to get at what's available in the library and on the Internet, the lack of funds continued to squeeze libraries. As with schools, seeking new avenues of financial support became routine in these decades for individual librarians, library boards of trustees, and taxing authorities.

Federal aid to libraries began in 1956 with the Library Services Act and continued with ESEA (with its provision for libraries) a decade later; subsequent legislation provided funds for rural, suburban, and urban libraries to put up buildings, add to collections, and offer expanded services, including the addition of new technologies. Yet federal dollars were, like federal aid to schools, helpful (in 1994, the federal share of total public library spending was 1.1%) but hardly sufficient to stave off cuts in staff and collections when economic recessions hit or public interest in supporting libraries flagged.[35]

The slow erosion of trust in public institutions that occurred in the wake of Vietnam and Watergate in tandem with economic downturns in the 1970s, 1980s, and 1990s spilled over into both libraries and schools in failing tax referenda and a growing belief—particularly after the dissolution of the Soviet Union—that a market-based society emphasizing choice, competition, and entrepreneurship was far superior to what government can do for its citizens. And libraries feeling the effects of staff cuts and seeking further efficiencies while looking for ways to increase patron visits and circulation—the coin of the realm in the world of public libraries—accommodated. Like school leaders seeing that market competition, innovation, choice, and entrepreneurial enterprise needed to be applied to public schools, librarians saw the same camel's nose under the tent.

As privately run bookstore chains expanded, adding coffeehouses and storytelling hours to their services, librarians felt the pinch of competition, and many turned to adopting market-based thinking: seeing patrons as customers, providing cafés and soft chairs, and offering new services such as partnerships with McDonald's and Starbucks or, as the new Salt Lake City glassy library did, building a mall-like array of gift, sandwich, and coffee shops.[36]

Not unlike schools under assault from critics who favored market-based solutions to governmental problems, libraries moved in a similar direction as they continued their traditional mission of cultivating literacy through free access to information, programming, and books, while still protecting the community's moral standards. As in the past, what information should be available to children and youth and the privacy of patrons' use of information became contentious political issues.

Even with frequent cutbacks in library budgets in these decades, distributing free information remained the reigning belief among professional librarians. New technologies helped considerably, in particular the advent of the personal computer.

COMPUTERS COME TO SCHOOLS AND LIBRARIES

Schools

Historically, schools have seldom been in the vanguard of embracing new technologies. Businesses and the military tended to be early adopters. So were libraries. Schools lagged behind in using technologies for instruction—from film, to radio, to television. Use of computers in schools for teaching, for example, began slowly in the early 1960s with computer-assisted instruction (CAI).

In the 1970s, the innovation required students to sit in front of terminals connected to mainframe computers and press keys to move through sequenced software programs in math and reading skills. For example, programmed software (or courseware) created by Computer Curriculum Corporation (CCC) spread during this period. Encouraging test results led to a flurry of corporations contracting with public school districts to teach reading and math to poor minority children in hopes that their skill levels would increase. By the early 1970s, however, the pay-for-performance contracts that used CAI had largely disappeared after scandals revealed cheating by particular firms. Still, in the 1970s and 1980s Jostens Corporation and CCC marketed Integrated Learning Systems (ILSs), or CAI dressed up in educational jargon. ILSs steadily expanded their markets in the 1990s, particularly in high-poverty urban and rural schools where tests scores were lower. By 2001, CCC reported that its courseware was in 16,000 schools, with 10 million students (one-fifth of total enrollment) tapping out answers to computer-asked questions. Even with these small inroads into the school market, adoption of new technologies was a painstakingly slow process.[37]

Entrepreneurs actively sought school markets for business-friendly policies. Apple's Steve Jobs lobbied for a federal bill in 1982 to put a computer in every school. The bill would permit hardware companies to donate machines to schools and write off taxes up to 200% of manufacturing costs—something that Congress had authorized the previous year for computer firms giving hardware to universities. The House of Representatives passed the bill, but it died in the Senate. A year later, when the California legislature passed a similar bill and the governor signed it into law, nearly 10,000 schools in the state received an Apple computer.[38]

Parents needed little convincing of technology's virtues when it came to their children using classroom computers. In their workplaces, cars, and supermarkets, chips in machines were everywhere. As personal computers made their appearance, media stories about children and computers infiltrated suburban parent's conservations. In 1982 *Time* magazine published its cover story "Here Come the Microkids" about children using software to program. One Michigan high school principal said, "Moms and dads are coming in and telling counselors they have to get their kids into computer classes because it is the wave of the future." In one 1998 poll, 79% of the respondents said computers would be "very helpful" in "teaching high-tech skills." When asked what they valued most about having computers in schools, 76% chose "students prepared for jobs" and 72% picked "students interested in learning." It was no surprise, then, that those parents prodded their neighborhood elementary school principals to get computers into classrooms.[39]

Nor did educators need much nudging from parents and media to go beyond CAI. Teachers, principals, school librarians, and superintendents were parents. They bought computers for their children and themselves. Moreover, public attention led administrators (and parents as well) to chase after business support. They echoed employer concerns about a skilled workforce and making students computer literate. As with business leaders, altruism and the value of public service easily got entangled with educators' self-interest. At the New Technology High School in Napa (California), for example, founding principal Robert Nolan said, "We want to be the school that business built." Walls of the renovated elementary school sported huge banners from Microsoft, Lotus, Hewlett Packard, and local business leaders. "This is not advertising," a New Technology High School administrator told a journalist, "this is a thank you from us to our partners."[40]

National leaders also joined local employers, parents, and educators in the crusade for more information and communication technologies (ICT) in schools. The massive shift in heavy manufacturing to other nations and the growth of knowledge-based industries made plain to U.S. presidents, state governors, and other elected officials the direction that both the economy and education would travel.

Between 1989 and now, three U.S. presidents styled themselves as "education" presidents and spent billions of federal dollars on wiring and hardware to make students technologically literate. "We know, purely and simply," President Bill Clinton said in 1996, "that every single child must have access to a computer, must understand it, must have access to good software and good teachers and to the Internet, so that every person will have the opportunity to make the most of his or her own life."[41]

In these years, school boards went on a virtual buying binge (enhanced by corporate donations and federal dollars). According to a 1984 survey, there were more than 125 students per computer in U.S. schools; in 2002, there were just below 4 students per computer. Schools wired for the Internet went from 35% in 1994 to 99% in 2002. Special high-tech schools multiplied across the nation. When home purchases of new technologies are considered, in 2000, over 67% of students lived in homes with at least one computer.[42]

Averages, of course, mask variation in access to ICT at home and school. According to a 2000 survey, about half of employed Americans under age 60 with incomes less than $30,000 a year use a computer at work. Of those earning more than $30,000 annually, four out of five use computers at work.[43]

While variation by income, race, and ethnicity still affects access for students—the so-called digital divide—that gap has shrunk considerably in the past decade. Nationally, the gap between students in poor and nonpoor schools has nearly disappeared, although regional differences still exist.

This picture of initially slow, uneven school adoption of new technologies for instruction, largely driven by external pressures, differs from the way that public libraries have embraced new technologies.

Libraries

Librarians have often been enthusiastic early adopters of new technologies in managing collections and serving the public. Decisions by library policymakers to automate cataloging and access to collections since the 1960s led naturally to librarians adopting desktop computers as they became available in the early 1980s and the Internet in the mid-1990s.

Professional librarians armed with degrees from graduate schools of information sciences were fully versed in bar codes, computerized collections, and finding creative ways of giving individual patrons the information they sought free of charge. Amid the conversion from print to nonprint and from books to cyberspace documents, the mission remained the same: advancing literacy, serving an increasingly diverse community, and guarding community standards.

By 2005 nearly every library in the nation offered free Internet access— a growth of 400% in less than 10 years. In the average library, there are just over 10 terminals available to the public. In the poorest neighborhoods, libraries offer the only chance to use the Internet. The three largest groups receiving both individual and group training in using ICT at libraries are seniors, persons without home computers, and adults seeking continuing education. Public libraries were doing a great deal to narrow the digital divide between the suburban haves and rural and urban have-nots.[44] The general public seems to expect the library to be the major community hub for computer and Internet access. As one woman said, "I don't go to the library very often. . . . If I'm going to go there, I'm going to do some kind of computer research or something. I think it's important that they have that."[45]

Like so many Americans, librarians embraced wireless technology, e-books, online tutoring, and book discussion circles. The Indianapolis–Marion County Public Library, for example, partnered with the local children's museum to offer "InfoZone" at the museum, where 20 computers house 15,000 books, CDs, videos, periodicals, and other sources. In Baltimore, the public library established Internet kiosks in shopping centers. And on and on.[46]

That's the good news of speedy adoption. The bad news is that nine out of ten librarians say the demand for more access to the Internet exceeds the supply. Funds are lacking for hardware and software upgrades and replacement of library computers.[47]

As before in the history of public libraries, continuing friction over the role of libraries in protecting children from pornography and other unwelcome online sites, exacerbated by the post-9/11 climate of fear about would-be or actual terrorists using the Internet to threaten public safety, occasioned federal legislation in the 1990s and since.[48]

In the age of cyberspace, two community institutions share a common mission of educating both adults and children. Both born in the heat of social movements to reform the nation's ills, their unswerving duty to serve communities for nearly two centuries has unfolded in different strategies because of fundamental differences between public schools and libraries in educating children and adults. One community institution is compulsory and committed to developing literacy, cultivating citizenship, preparing youth for the labor market, and strengthening moral character by teaching large numbers of children and youth for 180 days a year; the other community institution is voluntary for both adults and children and advances literacy, extends culture, guards morality, and serves the community by offering access to free electronic and print information. In trying to achieve their similar missions, generation after generation of reformers have continually sought to improve these core tax-supported institutions. When they have succeeded, few standing ovations or Academy awards greeted their efforts. When they failed, reformers lined up to point fingers, especially at schools, and offered their own solutions.

The next chapter goes beyond the easy explanation of differences in mission between libraries and schools to explain why these two community institutions, which acted as separated partners for decades, used different strategies and how those strategies influenced their adoption of technology.

CHAPTER 2

Explaining Libraries' and Schools' Different Strategies Toward Technology

So far, we have examined the adjacent planting of libraries and schools and their growth of common missions—to promote and guard literacy. They began as democratic equalizers, change agents, and guardians; they evolved as civic institutions that were and continue to be separated partners in promoting literacy. Although they have common missions, as Chapter 1 determined, they have pursued different strategies, especially toward technology. Why has that occurred? This question allows us to explore how it is that libraries and schools —similar community-based institutions with common missions for the public interest—adopted technology so differently in terms of type and speed.

While Chapter 1 focused on the social forces impinging on libraries and schools, in this chapter we discuss in detail the ways these institutions changed from the inside. We use institutional theory to assess the purposes, roles, and functions of libraries and schools and how these evolved to support and guard literacy. We then focus on ways that learning was formulated and used by each institution. Next, we focus on the diffusion and institutionalization of technology. In each section, we emphasize the key factors for school and library development, mentioned in Chapter 1, especially leadership and funding, to show ways they tried to balance their common mission with a dominant market-based ideology, making innovations both sustainable and relevant to society's political and economic goals.[1] Through a theoretical framework combining concepts drawn from institutional theory, adult learning, and diffusion of innovation, we offer an explanation as to why libraries embraced new technologies differently than did schools.[2]

PURPOSES AND ROLES

In the past four decades, scholars have come to see institutions as structurally reflecting the societal conditions they find themselves in. Yet institutions are hardly passive in responding to their immediate environment; they are active in creating social realities, and they do shape their surroundings. Richard Scott defines institutional theory broadly, as "processes by which structures, including schemas, rules, norms, and routines, become established as authoritative guidelines for social behavior [and] how these elements are created, diffused, adopted, and adapted over space and time," including how they decline and disappear.[3]

Using this definition, we focus on structural (formal roles and relationships), political (power, influence, and allocation of resources), human resources (skills and leadership), and symbolic (rituals, myths, shared values) aspects of institutions to highlight schools and libraries as places wrestling with innovations. Within this framework, we look closely at their different norms (such as rules, laws, culture), authority and legitimacy (the transmission of knowledge and skills), and professionalization (especially regarding gender), as well as the instructional roles of librarians and teachers that influenced technology adoption and use.

ISOMORPHISMS TO EXPLAIN THE CHANGE STRATEGIES OF LIBRARIES AND SCHOOLS

Libraries and schools have similar missions but use different change strategies in the communities they serve. This chapter explores the ways they cultivated one another (e.g., teachers guiding children to the library) and other civic institutions (e.g., newspapers, publishers, museums) to consolidate a culture of literacy.[4] For this reason, it is important to look at this problem ecologically—that is, as an "organizational field," a group of like-minded organizations that serve similar purposes—and examine the separate policies and practices of libraries and schools as they adapted to similar social and cultural forces. Paul Dimaggio and Walter Powell discuss three different types of institutional mechanisms, which they call isomorphisms, to explain how institutions in the same organizational field come to resemble one another. These mechanisms are important to understand when viewing the development of libraries and schools, their relationships to communities, and how they handled innovations from the progressive era to the present.

Organizational decision makers respond to external pressures by adjusting policies and practices. Why? According to some theorists, they do so because public and private organizations compete not only for resources and customers but also for political power and institutional legitimacy. As Powell and Dimaggio point out, "The concept of institutional isomorphism is a useful tool for understanding the politics and ceremony that pervade much modern institutional life" as well as frequent organizational change.[5]

There are three types of isomorphism. *Coercive isomorphism* occurs when organizations, especially ones that are dependent on other groups for resources, are compelled to adopt structures and rules in order to achieve legitimacy and, through political influence, to strengthen that legitimacy while conforming to legal mandates and social customs (e.g., the federal government requires that all public schools mainstream students with disabilities). *Normative isomorphism* occurs when organizations adopt certain structures because leaders believe they are the best ones and will lead to professionalization and wider acceptance (e.g., universities set professional norms in training lawyers, doctors, teachers, and managers). *Mimetic isomorphism* occurs when organizations copy one another (especially when one is viewed as more successful) in their response to uncertain circumstances, adopting innovations to enhance their legitimacy and provide solutions to difficult problems (e.g., U.S. companies borrowing quality control mechanisms from Japanese corporations in the 1980s). All three forms of isomorphism emerged during different historical periods in the evolution of libraries and schools and demonstrated their common purposes, albeit with different strategies as they interacted with the state and private companies.[6]

Between 1854 and 1918, libraries and schools were more susceptible to coercive isomorphism because of their dependence on reformers' wills and strong progressive ideology in conjunction with limited resources. Between the 1920s and 1970s, the normative period reigned as libraries and schools moved toward professionalism, attempting to gain credibility for their professions and the populations they served, accruing even more resources, especially from the government. The period since the 1980s can be characterized more as mimetic, as libraries and schools—during fiscal crises that threatened their identities—adopted similar innovations, viewpoints, and values and, as Chapter 1 made clear, moved in similar directions in embracing business models and the information-based economy.[7]

Although we present these isomorphic mechanisms of institutional change in neat packages by time periods, readers should recognize that there is much slippage in years and overlap among coercive, normative, and mimetic at any given time as environmental conditions shifted. Through these lenses, however, we can come to understand the evolution of schools and libraries with regard to their purposes, roles, and interests, as well as how they responded to similar social forces.

There are three important qualifications to make that relate to the limits of institutional theory and to the comparison of the development of schools and libraries. First, there is an ahistoricism about the relationship between these two institutions, leading us to contrive it—rarely are libraries discussed in school histories, and schools are featured only sporadically in the many library "house histories." Second, the institutions are unequal in that although libraries are as durable, there are fewer of them (about 16,000 libraries versus nearly 90,000 schools in 2005) and they are marginalized compared to schools in society.[8] Moreover, both schools and libraries perform many other roles—recreational, cultural, and informational—apart from education.[9] In fact, this ambiguity about libraries offering a broad range of services has been an advantage, expanding their boundaries, and a disadvantage, with the public, particularly the next generation, not understanding their mission.[10] This ahistoricism, marginalization, and multipurpose mission has led to tunnel visions and blind spots in the library field in terms of its identity and legitimacy as an educational institution.[11]

Third, although libraries, like schools, have developed as "systems," all libraries and schools are not the same. They differ in levels of resources, size, and location. Furthermore, library and school leaders, reformers, practitioners, and students and patrons have different goals and beliefs. Yet they are treated as homogeneous sets and mythologized by the many authors who glorify one over the other—from Mary Antin, who referred to the Boston Public Library as a "splendid palace" in her early 20th-century book, *The Promised Land,* to Irving Stone in the later 20th century, who said, "I think that the better part of my education, almost as important as that secured in the schools and the universities, came from libraries." Even educator John Taylor Gatto professes: "Those of you with a historical imagination will recognize Thomas Jefferson's prayer for schooling—that it would teach useful knowledge. Some places do: the best schooling in the United States today is coming out of museums, libraries, and private institutes."[12] As historian Harvey Graff states, not only are the uses of literacy and of libraries [and, we would add, schools] extremely variable and broad, but so, too, are the range of libraries [and schools] encountered and the mode of those encounters.[13]

Still, it is possible to gauge these institutions of literacy and learning that are "near the very heart of the complicated historical process, with all of the ironies, paradoxes, and contradictions that that implies" attending to *both* their structure and uses for literacy and learning over time.[14]

EARLY PERIOD: HIGHLY SYMBOLIC AND SYMBIOTIC (COERCIVE)

The years between the 1850s and 1870s focused on resources and development in libraries, while in schools the task was providing enough buildings and desks for those who enrolled. With few resources and even fewer patrons, libraries carried a more symbolic role, and reformers had a strong influence in establishing their credibility. In later decades, the 1880s to 1920s, libraries and schools developed together symbiotically—with different but nonetheless interrelated functions, with both schools and libraries taking on the task of Americanizing immigrants and supporting World War I. While schools received more public funding, libraries received major gifts from Andrew Carnegie and subsequently other wealthy benefactors, thereby growing a field and profession.

Symbolic

During their early period of growth, libraries and schools were instruments of social efficiency and self-improvement. As Andrew Carnegie stated, "The result of knowledge is to make men not violent revolutionists, but cautious *evolutionists*; not destroyers but careful *improvers*." Carnegie, viewed as a "patron saint" of libraries, gave money to build them in order to maintain the social order and as part of cultural reproduction. "My reasons for selecting public libraries," he said, "[are] that the true university of these days is a collection of books and that thus such libraries are entitled to a first place as instruments for the elevation of the masses of the people."[15]

As instrumental as these purposes were, however, schools were attracting more and more students after the Civil War, while libraries lacked patrons. In fact, Carnegie's grants were not for books. He gave money specifically for buildings, hoping to attract the public through a matched funding scheme whereby local leaders would underwrite a librarian as well as purchase books and materials. So the library had a symbolic purpose,[16] reflected in those classical library buildings with domes, monumental vistas, large rectangular rooms, rich front facades, and grandeur that characterized the "crown" George Ticknor described decades earlier and Antin's "kingdom in the slum"—all with the intention of bringing the high-culture canon of Western civilization to the masses.[17]

Yet shelves began to fill up with popular-culture materials in order to make it a useable, attractive, and nonintimidating institution to patrons. The library's legitimacy came through the book. The library transmitted and conferred legitimacy on library users through a faith that books would create an informed, enlightened, and educated citizenry.[18]

Librarians, largely middle-class women with an education and few other job prospects, were initially schooled to spread the "library spirit." Librarians were trained to catalog and collect materials and, when it came to people, to give what Samuel Green described in 1876 as a "personal touch" to bring them into the library. Melvil Dewey, for example, felt that the practice of librarianship depended on three traits: character, expertise, and institution. They were to be molded into "tender technicians." Their character and duties were to reflect the library as a place of order and rationality affiliated with state, religious, and commercial orders and, like schools, to achieve social ends.[19]

Melvil Dewey advised librarians to ensure that the collection included "the best books on the best subjects." If this occurred, Dewey said that "such a librarian will find enough who are ready to put themselves under his influence and direction, and if competent and enthusiastic, he may soon largely shape the reading, and through it his whole community." Dewey felt that this stimulation role could be performed best by women, for "to my thinking, a great librarian must have a clear head, a strong hand, and above all, a great heart. . . . and I am inclined to think that most of the men who achieve this greatness will be women." Green reiterated the importance of the fact that librarians be women—to woo patrons into the library through a kind of maternal guidance and cheerlead them into reading.[20]

So, as Dewey conceptualized, while "the library is a school and the librarian, in the highest sense a teacher," librarians were very limited in what they could do. Often trapped behind reference desks, they gave out information about where books were and recommended good reading. They attempted to establish good taste among serious readers and, for casual visitors, to instill a "faith" in books and reading as transformative. But they were never to advise patrons on substantive issues or reveal expertise that could be questioned by academic experts. The stereotypical Marion, or old-maid librarian with hair tied in a bun who has no real function other than to recruit patrons, still persists.[21]

While women numerically dominated the field, men led the American Library Association (ALA). At the same time, however, women's clubs were petitioning city fathers for Carnegie funding. Mayors were hesitant to transform private collections (not available to women) to public libraries, because Carnegie money had strings attached (to obtain building funds, cities had to allocate an annual budget worth 10% of the grant).[22]

As for schools in these years, teachers were responsible for direct instruction of groups of children 5 to 7 hours a day, unlike librarians answering patron questions. Teachers had slightly more autonomy in their classrooms—they could close their doors—than librarians did in answering patron questions and managing their collections.

Symbiotic

In the late 19th century, the closeness and even interdependence of libraries and schools were evident. Melvil Dewey claimed that "leading educators have come to recognize the library as sharing with the school the education of the people. . . . The school teaches them how to read; the library must supply them with reading which shall serve to educate." Schools were viewed as important for instilling basic literacy, while libraries could focus on furthering and reinforcing literacy practices through access to books. Libraries were also seen as a continuation of public schools, especially with few high schools available and high dropout rates among youth who did enroll.[23]

Librarians at this time agreed to this relationship. Mellen Chamberlain went further and argued that libraries could compensate for school weaknesses by taking advantage of library regularity, including operations (hours and days open to the public). Libraries also offered books to school districts when they were either in short supply or nonexistent, especially duplicate copies and for girls' reading in particular. They therefore should work together because "the public library is always in session, the School board once a month. . . . The library has what the school board has not—all of the force and speedy ordering, receiving and preparing books for use."[24]

Teachers were also encouraged to instill basic literacy in children, create lists of books, and help children find their way to the library. Yet the relationship was not without its frustrations. Librarians became frustrated with teachers and schools for not doing their part in inculcating literacy. As one librarian said, "Pupils in the public schools must first be taught how to read books before the library could perform its highest function to them." Moreover, frequent instructional reforms in schools were not viewed positively: "All these years are strewn with the wrecks of plausible inventions, short methods, and new-fangled notions, which, having come to grief leave the schools doing their work less efficiently, and producing as seems to be generally feared if not conceded, less valuable results than before."[25]

Of course, civic leaders viewed librarians as important for educating the immigrant parents of schoolchildren and connecting them to adult education agencies to give them more opportunities to learn English and study for citizenship tests. According to historian Phyllis Dain, during the late 1800s and early 20th century librarians subverted the aristocratic role and became cultural pluralists by engaging with immigrants as stakeholders, becoming intermediaries, and purchasing foreign-language collections. In essence, they made public library space more democratic. She viewed these commitments and practices as substantially different from those of schools, which, she said, "has been a formal, coercive, and collective experience, lending itself to the inculcation of standard values and information."[26]

These librarians also responded to new literacy demands in society by doing such things as holding classes and lectures on citizenship, bringing in native-language speakers, giving space to neighborhood families for planting gardens, and, in general, brokering educational linkages as advocates and social workers.[27]

As libraries searched for ways to maintain a stronger identity, the Library War Service Program (1917–1918) gave them a central function as 700 librarians sent as many as 7 million books to army post libraries constructed with Carnegie Corporation monies. Yet libraries, so tied to schools by a common literacy mission, played a subordinate role to schools as they mobilized children and parents to support U.S. soldiers at home and abroad. As one later report pointed out, "when once the [role] libraries play in the continuing process of education is recognized and understood, the library will be accorded its rightful place as an educational institution side by side with the school. Then, and not til then, will it be given its measure of public support." The library's lesser role in basic literacy provision—providing assistance but not teaching—and its performance as an auxiliary educational agency by providing materials and maintaining collections gave it a more passive community role, leading to a perception that it was mainly symbolic. The need was to create more professionalism, which would give it the same status as schools.[28]

MID-PERIOD: GROWTH OF THE PROFESSIONS (NORMATIVE)

Important institutional changes occurred in libraries and schools between 1920 and 1970. Both schools and libraries branched out in rural communities and in cities to reach more people. Schools had developed their own libraries, and teachers were becoming certified to staff school libraries. Universities developed academic libraries, leaving public libraries to forge their own expertise and separate professional identities. Not only did public libraries and schools expand but they also became more professionalized and efficient. Both institutions also sought linkages to the sciences, uniting progressive beliefs about the importance of democratic education and being secular, unlike churches, but more popular and more frequented than museums. Ranganathan's five "laws" of library science influenced librarians and stemmed from the library's new emphasis on reading and its purposes, apart from guarding morality. These were:

1. Books are for use.
2. Every reader has his or her book.
3. Every book has its reader.
4. Save the time of the reader.
5. The library is a growing organism.[29]

While public school champions sought "laws" such as these, they seldom found them. Nonetheless, in the beginning decades of the 20th century, public schools, especially urban districts, became increasingly centralized, bureaucratic, and professionalized. As part of the progressive reforms sweeping the nation, big-city school boards spurned political machines and refused to appoint their hacks to school boards. Reformers created nonpartisan boards composed of businessmen and professionals to govern schools. Reform-minded superintendents seeking efficiency and professionalism raised the qualifications for teachers and principals. States began to certify teachers and administrators. In-service training slowly became available. It was in these decades that school enrollments outstripped available buildings and new construction, tiny districts were consolidated, and larger numbers of college graduates were recruited for teaching and administrative positions. Efficient operations, progressive curricula, and multiple tracks in high school spread throughout the nation's cities. The Great Depression, however, considerably reduced funding of construction and salaries, although enrollments in high school mushroomed throughout the 1930s as older teenagers no longer dropped out to search for jobs, since few were available.[30]

The increasing centralization of both libraries and schools demanded efficient bureaucracies and professional credentials as well as training. Key reports in the 1920s funded by the Carnegie Commission and authored by ALA leaders identified deficiencies in the library field and signaled the need for federal involvement and funding to develop stronger professional organizations and education of librarians, especially in bibliographic instruction, reference, reading, and, most importantly, adult education. The library also needed to promote itself better. The public library still concentrated more on individuals and fostering their knowledge through reading.[31]

In library schools, general standards and theories of service were starting to develop. In the 1920s Jenny Flexner advocated that librarians be "sympathetic counselors" and stressed the importance of integrating new ideas in psychology with library work, and Malcolm Wyer promoted differing levels of reference service. Still, by the 1940s, attention remained on efficient methods of operating libraries and providing services to patrons. Schools in these decades concentrated on children's development, while libraries began to focus more on adults to the point where they seemed to be on separate educational tracks. As one observer noted, "They speak a different tongue and rarely understand each other." Library leaders urged that the library should be a "community educational establishment in all of its branches . . . a genuinely community university."[32]

This concept of the library as akin to universities (which were growing in number and had more status than schools) appealed to both library reformers and librarians. Plus, more and more adults were using the library as cities grew in population, especially during the Great Depression. Under Frederick Keppel, the Carnegie Corporation supported adult education through its grants to museums, evening schools, citizen councils, libraries, worker education programs, and correspondence schools. It underwrote surveys, publications, graduate education, and professional participation in associations. In 1938, Alvin Johnson called for the library to be a "people's university," echoing Dewey and other ALA leaders decades earlier but this time with an emphasis on adult education. The library would take on the civic roles of giving advice, supplying information, and becoming an education broker. Yet this expansive role did not go unchallenged. Many in the field opposed this direction for librarians.[33]

Despite these contradictions, during the 1920s and 1930s the library field saw the growth of its professional organization, the ALA, and its growing attachment to adult education and graduate education for librarians. Reader development was emphasized in library schools. This included acquiring in-depth knowledge of the collection, determining reading levels of patrons, making patrons comfortable, preparing lists of reading materials, interviewing readers casually, and following up on their progress. It also meant that records needed to be maintained to assess the librarians' activities and their impact on the public. With this focus and the sheer growth of more books on various topics, recreational reading bloomed during World War II.[34]

From the 1920s through the 1940s librarians concentrated on personal development, vocational improvement, and civic enlightenment. At this time, the ALA, whose stated objectives were to promote an "enlightened citizenry," championed the library bill of rights in 1948 (amended in 1961 and again in 1980) to advance democratic ideals. It included a code of ethics as well as statements about censorship, intellectual freedom, and the need to represent diverse viewpoints. Yet if the reading public was as middle-class as the Berelson 1949 report indicated, and if the library was to survive, according to advocates, it would have to open its doors wider and rely more on providing services and promoting citizenship than on just touting books.[35]

After World War II, librarians' concentration shifted from promoting reading to providing community and group services—reference and information, especially for vocational purposes—and to assisting war veterans with their readjustment. Programming for community groups shifted from labor organizations to women's and men's clubs. Book talks, exhibits, discussions, and displays, of course, continued with the Great Books discussions, begun in 1945 in Chicago. Moreover, the Ford Foundation started to pour money into libraries and to start programs on civic education and democracy.[36]

Despite librarians' training in adult education, several studies in the mid-1950s showed that their attitudes toward education and the role of the library in adult education were mixed. One 1954 study in particular revealed that most public libraries did not consider the needs of their communities in planning programs and that there was a need to train librarians. But such studies did not slow down the heavy funding by the Carnegie Corporation and Fund for Adult Education, which, in fact, helped start a flow of federal funding under the 1956 Library Services Act.[37]

The 1960s and 1970s also saw a much larger federal role for libraries and a tripling of money under the Library Services and Construction Act of 1965 to focus on low-income groups, urban and rural. The 1965 Adult Education Act also encouraged libraries to focus on low-income adults. Yet this agenda was contentious for both reformers and librarians. Proponents said it was the library's social responsibility to advocate for poor populations, and the Public Library Association (PLA) heavily supported this commitment since it fit with the historic educational mission of the library.[38] Opponents argued against these outreach services and experimental programs, saying that "the adult illiterate, however, does not need lots of books but rather one book. ... We must not be diverted by a misplaced sense of social responsibility into wasting resources on projects that are almost certain to disappear without a trace within a few years."[39]

While library leaders admonished librarians to get behind these efforts, it was a slow, hesitant process. "There are some librarians," one educator wrote, "who have been unhappy serving disadvantaged groups ... such an attitude, of course, presents a throwback to the time when libraries were mausoleums of silence and librarians were mainly guardians of books. We can only hope that such librarians will be forced to change their attitudes or that they will retire into silence they have held so golden." One 1966 study confirmed that librarian attitudes had changed little about their role as teachers or getting involved with poor populations.[40]

At the same time, library education was changing to accommodate new studies in psychology and sociology and a growing interest in adult learning. There was increased sensitivity in understanding the full range of patrons' emotions as they approached the reference desk and sampled culturally relevant programming. Librarians were taught how to give a comprehensive reference interview. Still, even with these changes, the librarian was not supposed to teach. Margaret Monroe, a leader in library adult education, asked: "Is it the library's role to teach?" Her answer: "It is the library's job to supply materials, and space for classes, recruit students and follow up with reading guidance and information service to adult new literates." And that is exactly what librarians did with their experimental programs in the 1960s and 1970s. In essence, the library saw itself as a community sponsor.[41] However, decreased funding in the 1970s made it difficult to fully realize this goal.[42]

For public schools in these decades, many changes also occurred around professionalization and working with new populations. The civil rights movement spilled over into public schools, generating concerns about the effects of poverty and segregation on both Whites and minorities. Federal action to reduce inequalities between the poor and middle class, between minorities and Whites, led to the Elementary and Secondary Education Act (1965), which sent monies into poor communities for the first time. Disillusion with big-city school districts and their bureaucracies and a desire to shake loose from mind-stifling regulations led to movements for alternative high schools, community control of local schools, and a storm of innovations hyped to cure the ills of urban and rural poor schools. Efforts to entice schools, teachers, and students into more community involvement sprang up in cities, suburbs, and rural areas. Concerns about dropouts and low literacy generated new and experimental programs inside and outside public schools. Newly minted projects popped up in cities: "Free high schools," "open classrooms," and "community-controlled schools" became featured topics in news articles and subjects of television programs as educators sought reforms that would end the poor academic performance of minority students.[43]

By the mid-1970s, however, the human and fiscal costs of the war in Vietnam, the Watergate scandals, a civil rights movement in the doldrums, and an economic downturn had wiped out much of the energy and élan of the prior decade. The optimistic belief of policymakers, teachers, researchers, and parents that schools could solve social problems soured into a lethargic pessimism about what schools could achieve. Tougher preparation for college and raising academic standards by passing a test to graduate from high school became "new" features of post-1960s schooling.[44]

For libraries, the late 1970s saw a rethinking of the library mission and its future, especially as the federal funding of Great Society programs shifted to revenue sharing under Presidents Nixon and Reagan. Nixon, for example, more than halved library program funding. The 1979 ALA *Mission* statement concluded: "The nation's public libraries are in serious trouble." Enter computers.[45]

LATE PERIOD:
CHANGING FOR COMPETITION (MIMETIC)

When the *Nation at Risk* report in 1983 warned of the possible decline of the U.S. economy unless the educational system embraced the new knowledge-based economy, libraries and schools heeded the alarm. Yet in this era of increased pressure from all sides, private and public, there was also considerable confusion about how to produce the intended effects. One thing that was certain was that in a customer-driven market, both institutions had to prove that their resources and services were delivered efficiently. They were charged with delivering services cheaply and using outcome measures to determine success. Business models started to creep in as increased standardization and accountability systems became important in proving their public worth to taxpayers. Although computers were being used in the 1970s in libraries for technical processes and for improving workflows like cataloging and bibliographic organization, it wasn't until the 1980s, with the stress on collecting information and accountability, that an infrastructure of computers was used for recordkeeping and networking. Later, in the 1990s, technology was being used for more diverse purposes, including instruction, databases, document delivery, digital library collections, e-books and e-journals, and, most importantly, connectivity to the World Wide Web.

From the 1980s onwards, both libraries and schools began to adapt to workforce demands in what was seen as a swiftly emerging information-based economy. Logistical reasons also influenced the turn to administrative technology in libraries. The dire need to better manage the sheer explosion of information and records with less space and money that began in the mid-20th century led to libraries adopting cooperative acquisitions, fee-based services, and outsourced cataloging. In schools, administrative uses of computers (e.g., for personnel, purchasing, student data) also began in the 1960s and spread rapidly in large school districts and states. The lure of higher productivity convinced school boards and superintendents to purchase computers and use the new technologies to automate common administrative tasks—but not for instruction. Except for a spurt of activity around computer-assisted instruction in math and reading in elementary schools, little activity occurred in classrooms before the mid-to-late 1980s. In schools, computers were sold to boost basic academic skills.[46]

Significantly, in the 1980s, libraries adopted online catalog systems for patrons, now referred to as "users." Librarians learned how to help users, through bibliographic instruction, to gain both "information literacy" (knowledge of information resources) and "library literacy" (knowledge of library resources). During this period, library schools, with their changed names that included the word *information*, began to see librarians as "information intermediaries" or "information counselors" teaching "bibliographic instruction." With quantifiable information data, it would be possible to focus more on discrete outcomes. A whole literature emphasized inputs/outputs and outcomes.[47]

Yet when studies in the mid-1990s started to show that many libraries were not connected to the Internet, federal officials and private foundations paid more attention to connecting these library users. The Gates Foundation made substantial gifts to the nation's public libraries, and the Library Services and Construction Act of 1995 (the name was changed to Library Services and Technology Act in 1996) provided funding for libraries in low-income areas to purchase more computer hardware and software. Then, in 1996, President Clinton authorized libraries to be moved from the U.S. Department of Education to Museum Services, thereby encouraging a new cultural focus and opening the door for fee-based services. This was done despite earlier studies showing that low-income and minority patrons, more than Whites and those with higher incomes, felt the "educational role" of the library was "very important." Both populations wanted computers *and* books.[48]

Library leaders encouraged high technology as a public good and thought of this as the "new paradigm" incorporating business models and privatization. According to these business-oriented proponents, libraries should be managed like corporate-owned bookstores. With these changes, a few voices complained that libraries would forget books: "Tote that rice, lift that Grisham," one reader wrote in an editorial, emphasizing that "the mission of the bookstore is to make money." The reader, a former bookseller, went on to write, "Service is a priority only insofar as it affects the bottom line . . . morale [is] low and turnover high [at places like Barnes and Noble]."[49]

Most librarians were not worried about being replaced by business-driven managers; they saw themselves as strong professionals and key players in the nation's new information infrastructure as it attracted new funds, preached equality, and expanded access to information. Moreover, ALA leaders endorsed the public library as an information safety net. They advocated helping people find information and gaining skills for the new workforce. Yet there was some identity confusion.

In 1998, the ALA asked its membership: "Purveyors or prescribers: What should librarians be?" One librarian replied:

> I don't think there is any common understanding of what an education institution is among libraries and the word education itself can have all sorts of different meanings.

Librarians exclaimed: "Herein lies our problem, we have no clearly established hierarchy of professional values."[50]

In addition, demographers predicted that many of the current generation of librarians would retire by 2015. Replacements needed to look younger, and be more tech-savvy, than those retiring. New descriptors for librarians emerged, such as "ambassadors, technology experts, and human search engines." One librarian boasted that patrons say to her, "You don't look like a librarian . . . it doesn't fit you at all"; another stated that the ALA should run advertisements that "librarians are hot." Leaders welcomed the growing interest in the image of librarians as a move toward attracting those in information management schools who would be wooed by corporate salaries. "The competition is not just financial," said library educator, Leigh Estabrook. "Businesses and Microsoft pay a lot better than most public libraries, but they also offer our students corporate nonlibrary jobs."[51] A few library educators criticized the role of technology in public libraries and its bond to the postindustrial society as simply "following the money." By the 1990s, state support for library funding had severely declined, especially in western states (aside from Hawai'i and Alaska), while public schools fared better.

Schools sought private funding, as did libraries. This dire need for funds made technology more appealing as an efficiency move that would cut costs. But neither information nor technology were seen by critics as "neutral tools" that librarians or teachers were uncritically adopting. Critics pointed out that schools and libraries were heeding the demands of a market economy; they were bargaining because of an ambiguous and insecure future.[52]

In these years, public schools were also pressed by state and federal officials to adopt business-inspired school reforms so that students would be prepared for a highly competitive economy. Corporate and civic leaders joined coalitions of the willing who sought to raise academic standards; determine by tests whether students met those standards; and hold schools, teachers, and students responsible for achieving the desired outcomes. Employers sought high school and college graduates who could enter jobs with an array of hard and soft skills that would keep companies competitive in a global economy. Test-based accountability spread throughout the nation's schools, culminating in President George W. Bush's signature legislation, No Child Left Behind.

The law pressed educators to raise every student's achievement to proficiency in reading, math, and other subjects by 2014 or face the consequences of schools being taken over, reconstituted, or some combination of penalties. School officials turned to new technologies, parental choice of charter schools, developers of whole-school reform, professional development, and for-profit organizations that promised gains in academic achievement.[53]

With such demands placed on schools and libraries, the mimetic isomorphism that we mentioned earlier emerged in full display. From the 1980s onwards, copying business practices to improve library and school productivity is the obvious incarnation of mimetic isomorphism. In our minds, libraries and schools traveled similar paths in responding to their environment in later decades. The presence of computers in libraries and schools needed to be further validated through learning doctrines that validated its purpose in postindustrial society.

LEARNING IN LIBRARIES AND SCHOOLS: LIFELONG LEARNING FITTED TO THE KNOWLEDGE-BASED ECONOMY

The pragmatic approaches that characterized the changes over the years in both libraries and schools filtered into the ways these institutions treated learning for both adults and children. In the early periods, we saw that libraries focused on self-education and self-improvement through reading books, while schools concentrated on inculcating basic values and cultivating literacy. By the 1940s, the progressive mind-set of the whole child, active learning, connecting school to real life, and democratic practices had permeated educators' vocabularies and entered the public consciousness. Crisply expressed by John Dewey, who said that "real education comes after we leave school and there is no reason why it should stop before death," learning was recognized as occurring in homes and communities, not just schools, and across the lifespan. But the concept was respected more in words than in practice, and neither institution formally recognized the other as a partner in extending learning opportunities. Schools concentrated on children's development, whereas libraries focused on adults and embraced the idea of adult education. Adult education gave way to the new–old concept of lifelong learning in the 1960s and then, later, the Learning Society, as the perception grew that economic, technological, and communication trends were shrinking the world and current education was constricted and short-sighted. Although lifelong learning remained in educators' and librarians' vocabulary and was repeated by business leaders, it clearly played a secondary role to tying libraries and schools to market competitiveness.[54] Moreover, the language of workforce training for the knowledge-based economy was more popular and emphasized the importance of computers in both institutions.

Libraries

Since the 1960s, adult education has merged into lifelong education and learning. Foreshadowed in the 1920s by William Learned and other adult education reformers, library proponents wanted to give adult education credibility and separate it from children's development. In 1929, one supporter affirmed: "The purpose of adult education is to prevent adult starvation, not to compensate for lack of schooling in youth."[55] Leaders, like Margaret Monroe, championed the library as an "adult learning center" and invited in adult educators Malcolm Knowles and Cyril Houle. "For what purposes does the American public library exist?" Houle asked. His answer: "All of the purposes are educational in one sense or another, and the library, by making these opportunities available, can properly be called, an agency of adult education."[56]

Yet many of these independent learning ideas were seen as separate from subsequent federally funded programs for the urban and rural poor. Although early leaders, like Helen Lyman, advised librarians to design literacy programs according to adult learning principles, in practice many of these programs did not use these principles. Yet these programs did benefit from the many adults who volunteered their time to tutor with the founding in 1960 of the Laubach method and, in 1962, Literacy Volunteers of America.[57]

By the 1980s, libraries and schools were increasingly viewed as "learning organizations" and displayed a strong drive toward innovation, endorsing business-inspired organizational management. Library leaders urged professionals to embrace technology because of its dominating presence within, as the slogan ran, the Learning Society. In 1986, one librarian educator concluded that "no aspect of life is [un]affected by the combination of social and technological forces and it is unrealistic to adopt an ostrich-like stance, ignoring the certain reality of both change and its acceleration pattern."[58]

Increasingly, many librarians viewed lifelong learning as enhancing employ-ability instead of just personal development.

This emphasis on never-ending learning gained greater visibility with the 1983 *Nation at Risk* report. While the report scorched U.S. public schools for their mediocrity, it encouraged libraries to join in the global race for economic supremacy. A year later, library leadership addressed this issue in: "Public Libraries and Excellence: The Public Library Response to a *Nation at Risk*," which acknowledged the fiscal constraints facing libraries and stressed the need for libraries to "link their resources to help create a learning society."[59]

Literacy efforts in libraries were prized insofar as they could produce measurable outcomes and make the library more visible. Computers would assist this effort. By 1986, 218 grants had been given to local libraries to acquire hardware and software to promote literacy. Yet most of this was seed money rather than maintenance money, and much of this was not for direct instruction in literacy.[60]

By the 1990s, librarians were promoting information literacy as it re-lated to the new economy. The 1991 White House Conference on "Library and Information Services for Productivity, Literacy, and Democracy" ex-amined the role of libraries, business, and government in collaborating to build literacy skills among workers. Part of this call for new technologies in libraries accompanied requests for increased funds from private donors such as Bill Gates, who would provide much needed software to increase information access—a goal championed by the ALA yet whose leaders fully understood that local taxes rather than federal funds paid for libraries. In 1990, the ALA also adopted the policy "Library Services for the Poor," to expand literacy services. By the end of the century, literacy services had spread to nearly 90% of all public libraries, with computers taking over the programs.[61]

At the same time, libraries did not want to lose their middle-class base and be linked only to "traditional literacy" for immigrants and poor patrons. For this reason, the ALA adopted information literacy and linked it to life-long learning and literacy. As one brochure put it: "Helping people of all ages to be savvy consumers of information is becoming an increasingly im-portant part of what libraries and librarians do."[62]

Money, of course, mattered. In the early 1990s, a U.S. National Com-mission of Libraries and Information Science (NCLIS) study found that in 9,050 of the nearly 16,000 public libraries, only 20% had access to the Internet and that federal assistance was needed. Moreover, additional mon-ies were needed to underwrite the infusion of technology into libraries through the National Research and Education Network (NREN). The purpose of NREN was to wire libraries in rural and low-income schools so that anyone could access the Internet. Yet library operating budgets were not keeping pace with the costs of installing and maintaining new technologies, and print materials cost more each year—currently federal taxes account for only 1% of library budgets. Turning to the private sector and charging user fees of patrons seemed to make sense. In such a fiscal climate, foundation and library partnerships were seen as "natural," with the rationale dating back to the early years of Andrew Carnegie's gifts.[63]

Funding streams, competition with other institutions, and privatization forces influenced new technologies' rapid diffusion in libraries as a learning tool, highlighting the leading function of libraries as learning and information service providers in society. Public support for these roles was strong, as a 1996 Benton Foundation survey found. *Buildings, Books, and Bytes* noted that a majority of all Americans, especially minorities, valued the library as a place to get information through computers and online services. Ten years later, another report, *Long Overdue*, funded by the Gates Foundation, reached the same conclusion. From the 1990s onwards, monies for technology flowed from the private sector to libraries, with the Gates Foundation being the most notable private source ($250 million) since Andrew Carnegie's gifts. Gates's monies account for the spread of computers in libraries serving low-income patrons.[64]

Literacy program staff, seeing their federal funding base drying up, sought private funding. The Wallace Foundation–ALA initiative pumped $4 million into literacy programs during this period. Further financial support came from the federal Library Services and Technology Act, Verizon, and many other small and large communication and retail companies. The link to skills-based training was intentional as ALA started to address workforce literacy issues explicitly and received grants to make literacy learning more business-friendly. Computers were billed as "tireless and nonjudgmental" teachers, and programs were called "computer-assisted" and "learner-centered." Most library literacy programs emphasized technology as curriculum (that is, gaining tech skills) and as a complement to instruction (that is, use of commercial software). Much of this was due to the independent learning emphasis of the library and the lack of professionals to teach reading and writing, including a constant lack of tutors. These programs became more and more dependent on computers for instruction.

Librarians' roles as mediators and stimulators, joined to the idea of the library as an "alternative community learning center," complemented this trend. Since there were few if any accountability standards for computer use and learning, libraries could capitalize on any unintended effects of learning technologies and were seen as reflecting the largely experimental role libraries were playing with computers.

Many adult learners reported they were attracted to library literacy programs specifically because they were not designed like schools and had the library atmosphere of personalized service. These programs, in contrast to other adult education agencies, were some of the first in many communities to house many computers, much software, and extensive lab resources. While other local adult education agencies struggled to gain access to computers for both students and teachers alike, the public library provided computers for literacy instruction. Moreover, the public and learners alike favored the self-pacing, individualization, immediate feedback, privacy, and practice features of the educational software.[65]

Librarians sought to become leaders in the information and communication revolution, and they needed to market their informational roles to survive. "Librarians," one advocate said, "should seize more recognition—and the support that comes with it."[66] The American Library Association promoted 21st-century literacy through "technology for outreach and innovation."

Schools

For public schools, on the other hand, the process of adapting new technologies to administrative tasks moved swiftly but slowed considerably when applied to classroom instruction. School administrators automated central office tasks such as purchasing, personnel, and test score analysis. Business- and parent-driven demands for schools to get wired for the Internet and to purchase the latest hardware and software moved schools to develop the infrastructure for teacher and student use of computers. New technologies were deployed to classrooms, labs, media centers, and mobile carts. Regular use of computers for instruction in reading, math, and other academic subjects, however, moved at a measured and deliberate pace. There was more computer access and use in high schools than in elementary schools and more computer use in English than in math. Few literacy-based technology programs, however, either captured the school curriculum or dominated instruction. While a few teachers and principals pioneered in adopting and using new technologies for teaching and learning, most practitioners did not see their success as dependent on how much or how often they used machines in their schools and classrooms.

While forms of institutional isomorphism and adult learning theories may account for the appearance of instructional technology in schools and libraries, neither accounts for the differing rates of and types of adoption in libraries and schools. Diffusion theory helps deepen our understanding of this phenomenon.

DIFFUSION OF NEW TECHNOLOGIES INTO LIBRARIES AND SCHOOLS

Under the influence of pro-business approaches and external pressures to accommodate to a knowledge-based economy (discussed above), libraries and schools developed similar structures in the waning decades of the 20th century receptive to privatization and new communication and instructional technologies. Adoption did happen, but it did so differentially in terms of speed and type—libraries were faster and their computer usage was more fully adapted to the institution.

The diffusion process can be defined as the spread of things that are new or perceived as new by members of a social environment and that are called "innovations." Everett Rogers defined the diffusion process as consisting of four elements: (1) the innovation and then (2) communication from one individual to another (3) in a social structure and (4) over time. The social structure contains communication networks, which spread the innovation, and is essentially a social system composed of individuals (top decision makers as well as practitioners) solving problems in their different roles, who adopt the innovation over a period of time. Let's look at the social structures of libraries to see why they are more accommodating to technology—the innovation—and how it spread so much more easily in libraries than in public schools.[67]

Trend Toward McLibraries

In a more competitive climate for funds and patrons, libraries promoted a new customer-based model of service, managerial efficiencies, and fee-based structures to attract more public support, particularly from middle-class and business-minded patrons. Libraries were competing with bookstores and Internet purchases while also responding to demands for productivity from municipal authorities. "Executives who are apt to have read more management books than literature" looked at partnerships with Starbucks and McDonald's as ways to "creatively" fund libraries. Librarians chose mass-marketed books and, in many cases, these choices were outsourced to intermediary profit-seeking organizations.[68]

In libraries, the coffee shops and bookstores were considered "value-added." This trend toward infotainment, critics argued, hurt serious readers of books by focusing instead on "graphic skills, storytelling techniques . . . the music [and] marketing strategies; in fact the whole compelling panopoly of the entertainment industry."[69] In addition, as John Buschman points out, the customer-driven librarianship model brought a numbers-driven accountability similar to that of Starbucks or bookstores that was linked to funding. Libraries needed to be less library-like. The concept of "libraries without walls," with a central role for computers, seemed to make libraries sleek information superhighways or infotainment centers—"learning and leisure centers" to attract users, particularly the middle class.[70]

While the customer model hit schools, too, especially the emphasis on personal computers, governance and organizational structures have disallowed a more complete merging with business models. Many factors have slowed the adoption and spread of information technologies in classroom instruction. A decentralized system of schooling involving 15,000 school districts and 90,000 schools surely played a role in slowing down the spread of any innovation. Public schools, moreover, have social, economic, political, and academic purposes that serve both individuals and society. Taxpayers expect schools to create literate adults, build citizens engaged in democratic practices, socialize the young, and prepare youth for the workplace while inculcating basic moral values and strengthening character. Parents also expect that their daughters and sons who finish schooling will earn a decent living and rise in social status. Furthermore, schools have been drafted continually to solve national problems: in 1954, desegregation; in the late 1950s, via the National Defense Education Act; in the 1990s, via legislation getting more technologies into schools to prepare the next generation of workers for an information-based workplace.[71]

Even with these disparate and complex purposes and mounting economic and social pressures from business-inspired reformers, parents worried about their children's employment futures. While many educators were early adopters of new technologies in the mid-to-late 1980s after the introduction of the personal computer, classroom uses of new technologies lagged considerably behind and can be attributed to the above factors. Since the late 1980s and especially with the onset of the Internet in the mid-1990s, school boards have spent enormous amounts of public and private funds to wire and equip schools to give all teachers and students access to new technologies. Nonetheless, after two decades of purchases and wiring, teachers and students use computers in classrooms for instruction far less than promoters have sought.

Trend Toward Deprofessionalization in Libraries

While libraries were changing from the inside to "follow the money" by adopting more technology and privatization schemes, professional library schools also changed. University library schools, for example, changed their names and merged with information, media, and computer science departments to attract candidates who could work in many more kinds of libraries and in private industries.

Not just in name did libraries change; they shifted in mission also. One of the reforms of the ALA's Committee on Accreditation allowed for each school to define its own mission and be evaluated on those terms. As a result, the number of professors in graduate schools who had worked in public libraries dropped and nonlibrarians were sought who then would become faculty teaching novice librarians. The problem, according to one librarian, was that these nonlibrarians "have never worked a day in their lives in a real library." One writer, tongue in cheek, recommended not displaying the library school diploma because "people who work in libraries do not put much stock in library schools." In order to save money in libraries on staff, many paraprofessionals and nonprofessionals were hired. The high-tech identity crisis in professional schools and public libraries was eloquently framed by Theodore Roszak, who said, "Maybe libraries no longer need walls, maybe walls no longer need libraries, maybe librarians no longer need books, maybe librarians no longer need librarians." He, like librarians themselves, believes that librarians have critical and generalist knowledge of electronic sources in a way that nonprofessionals do not, in addition to being "guardians of literacy" along with teachers.[72]

According to some educators, there has been a deskilling movement, whereby librarians do not own their information, work processes, or fee structures and have lost control over their jobs. One example is the recent partnership between Google and the New York Public Library, which has agreed to digitize much of its collection. But this partnership has caused librarians to worry that this information will be priced for sale and thus betray the historic mission of giving patrons free access to materials.[73]

Much of this rapid diffusion of technology and copying of corporate practices is related to management hierarchy, whereby top administrators often make technology decisions. As one critic put it, "Downsizing, outsourcing . . . an increase in temporary and part-time employment. . . . These practices are often attributed to automation or computerization, but they really result from the management decision to use automation to contain or reduce labor costs than to improve services." Aping the private sector—what we earlier called mimetic behavior—swiftly spreads these practices.[74]

Such changes also skew gender relations among staff. While about 80% of librarians are women, less than half are administrators; women make up less than half of all faculty in library schools. Moreover, women hold more of the part-time positions. The need to improve the image of librarians and libraries has meant attracting more men to the field, both as patrons and as librarians. According to Sarah Pritchard, there is a false myth that public libraries are unfriendly to men. Librarianship, she states, "has an image problem because women have an image problem. The answer is not to bring more men or computers to the field. The answer is to improve the status of women in society."[75]

But that is hard to do if library professional work becomes routinized. Roma Harris's[76] deskilling theory holds that technological displacement threatens women's professional position, whereby knowledge workers become data workers, evidenced by a decline in public librarians throughout the 1980s, "which may be computer-related." She contrasts professional work, which is nonroutine, to automated services, which make it easier to hire nonprofessionals. In such instances, management has more control over the pace and nature of work. Such deskilling is most obvious in cataloging, selection, and reference services, where, for example, online searching is now referred to as "end-user searching" as more responsibility for finding information is passed on to patrons. All of these managerial decisions about staffing, automation, and deskilling quickly diffuse new technologies throughout the institution. Some librarians see the rapid spread of automation and new practices as an escape from the "occupational heritage" and, most importantly, the commitment to public service, which is at the heart of librarians' identity. Others see the swift embrace of technologies as enhancing the profession.[77]

ADOPTION PROCESSES OF LIBRARIES AND SCHOOLS

Rapid adoption of technology is viewed among many librarians and school practitioners as increasing the status of the profession. Being high-tech in 21st-century America is highly prized. Libraries are especially able to serve as an "electronic safety net" based on their professional goals, "creating a level playing field between public and private interests." Librarians, in this new competitive environment, are instructed to be "politically savvy" and use their historic role to their advantage in addressing the needs of minority users, building partnerships with other agencies, and using technology to preserve a community's culture.[78]

Similarly, in schools with computer labs scattered through the building and mobile carts filled with laptops available to teachers, administrators can point with pride to the spanking new machines even if they are only occasionally used by most teachers. Symbolically, schools must have icons of modernity to reassure taxpayers that they are up to date and that computers are available to help students ease into the labor market after graduation.

In summary, institutional theory helps to account for the common conditions of technology within schools and libraries as they adapted to economic, political, and social forces. Libraries adopted businesslike reforms, which fit with their purpose and roles. Librarians have come to focus on customer-service models, with new technologies infiltrating every aspect of their daily work with patrons, to maintain a niche in a competitive market while serving as a safety net for the public—eliminating the digital divide through their tech-savvyness. Libraries, in competing with businesses, needed to gain status as key players because industry is threatening their very existence, causing angst about their future roles. Yet there was not a huge transition because the need was prevalent, the conditions were ripe, and the payoffs were promising. The public rewarded libraries with more visits as soon as they were wired to the Internet, up 17% from 1996 to 2001.[79]

In these years, learning for the purpose of succeeding in the workforce took hold in both libraries and schools. While both focused on computer-based and computer-assisted learning early on for improving skills, libraries turned more to automated learning because it was cheaper, more efficient, and complemented its traditional role as well as its future one as an information broker.

While school reformers pushed a business model, new information and communication technologies seldom came to dominate most classrooms because of the school's other social and political responsibilities to inculcate in children far more than information literacy. Schools also sought to teach children how to behave in groups, become active citizens, and act responsibly in communities.

Librarians could be seen as early adopters because of their accommodating structures and purposes, while teachers, who work within different structures and have many other nontechnological purposes, are often seen—unfairly—as laggards.

The institutional isomorphisms, learning, and diffusion theories help explain the differential entry and spread of new technologies in schools and libraries. Up until this point, we have concentrated on explaining how these institutions, guardians and promoters of literacy, performed their societal roles by adopting new technologies. The next two chapters will focus more on learners' uses of instructional technology.

CHAPTER 3

Libraries, Literacy, and Instructional Technology

Library literacy programs exemplify the library's social responsibility and literacy mission. These programs attract new markets and new technologies through private and public funds and pioneer the customer-driven, self-improvement, and lifelong learning model that reflects modern library services. This chapter examines the history of library literacy programs by taking a close look at those literacy programs that use technology and discusses their implications for libraries and adult learners.

A BRIEF HISTORY OF TECHNOLOGY-BASED LIBRARY LITERACY PROGRAMS

Literacy was wedded to 19th-century reformers' desires for self-improvement and to librarians' professional responsibilities to create a reading public. The purpose of the earliest literacy services was to help immigrants in the early 20th century adapt to mainstream American culture.[1]

The next peak period for literacy programs was in the 1960s. Although there were reading programs for adults in the mid-1950s, it wasn't until President Lyndon B. Johnson's War on Poverty in the mid-1960s that libraries began providing services specifically for those who were marginalized in society and considered "illiterate" or "disadvantaged." Many of these programs were for immigrants and the native-born, in rural and urban settings. These programs were used to widen the entryway for nontraditional clients and to attract different groups that had not previously entered libraries.[2] Libraries offered their own tutoring as well as space for other literacy programs to tutor, recruited volunteer tutors, did referrals to other agencies, maintained large-print and literacy-related materials and books, and promoted other literacy-related activities in the community.

As these programs matured, they began to widen their scope to include immigrant communities and, with the American Library Association's (ALA) promotion, to get new readers into libraries. The ALA advertised literacy as a natural and historical purpose of libraries because of this whole-community focus. Librarians were called on to build their collections with high-interest, low-level reading materials, refer new readers to local agencies, publicize their services, and provide meeting space for tutors.[3]

By the 1980s, however, research studies showed that librarians were hardly involved in literacy instruction. They provided literacy services that fit most squarely with the library's role—collecting books, referring, and giving out space. Researchers found that only 25% of libraries offered literacy programming, and this seemed to be based on whether or not other community agencies were offering this service.[4] During this time, there were sporadic efforts by librarians to bridge gaps between libraries and local and national literacy agencies. By mid-decade, spurred by federal grants, existing library literacy programs diversified to include programs on technology, family literacy, and English for Speakers of Other Language (ESOL).[5]

The National Literacy Act, passed in 1990, stressed that libraries should coordinate with other community-based agencies. Literacy services in most public libraries came to be considered a "community anchor." Yet libraries' major approaches continued to be "passive services," that is, providing space, giving referrals, and maintaining collections rather than direct tutoring. This was not considered acceptable to library leaders, as a new study—the National Adult Literacy Survey of 1993—had shown there were 40 million adults with very low literacy levels in the nation. Many library and literacy leaders called for increased and intensified library involvement with literacy to rectify this problem.

Even though library literacy programs best represented the library's original mission, they remained on the periphery compared to other library core services like reference. Often funded by grants and run by nonlibrary staff, literacy programs were considered "special projects" by most librarians. Proponents called for greater coordination of libraries in their communities to promote literacy, especially as a community-based development effort.[6]

Library literacy program professionals, struggling to enter the core of library services, were eager to integrate technology because it would unite them with the library's embrace of automation and desire for a technological makeover. Computers would draw more people into the library, increasing building use and circulation figures as well as assisting with instruction (due to the lack of tutors). Computers would also attract interest from corporate and foundation donors, giving the library a niche for business partnerships. Furthermore, with a workforce emphasis, library literacy programs could also attract employment and welfare agencies, which would give the library strong links to community agencies. Furthermore, these adult learners would come in handy for libraries during funding crises, when they could provide testimonials about how much the library had helped them in improving their reading skills and gaining workplace skills, thus raising the library's profile.[7]

By the 1990s, adult literacy's profile was more visible but was viewed in a more mechanized way than in earlier decades. On the front cover of the May 1997 issue of *American Libraries*, for example, an adult learner is pictured as a funnel, with letters pouring into its top and "literacy" emerging from its bottom. In the same journal a year later, an illustration of a working man has the title "retooling literacy for the 21st century." Literacy programs moved from an emphasis on access to education in the 1960s, to literacy programming in the 1980s, to showing literacy skill outcomes for the workforce by the 1990s.[8]

The trend toward workforce literacy was reinforced through an ALA initiative called "What Works." The White House Conference on Libraries in 1991 focused on literacy and the formation of a productive workforce in public and private sectors. One advocate argued that successful library literacy programs needed to obtain private grants and turn more to computers as a tool for both learning and for their survival during major budget cuts. This privatized/business framework was picked up in "Family Literacy Programs Make ene," an article in *The Bottom Line* promoting family literacy in order to save money on programs by partnering with "companies and businesses which have never before given to a publicly supported institution . . . [and encouraging] private benefactors who have never before donated to a library to come forth and want to contribute" (p. 49).[9]

A strong economic rationale for workforce development with computers and technology at its center emerged in library literacy programs for families and individuals alike. What's more, a multimillion-dollar grant by the Wallace Foundation to improve library literacy programs through building computer labs reinforced the links between workplace literacy and technology, representing a gateway for workers. By the early 21st century, nearly all library literacy programs contained computers as a dominant form of instruction and as a promising tie-in with the labor market and the knowledge-based economy. How did new information and communication technologies win such swift acceptance?

THE IMPORTANCE OF COMPUTERS IN LIBRARY LITERACY PROGRAMS

Federal and private agencies have played a large role in introducing and promoting technology in library literacy programs since the 1980s. The appeal of modernity in high-tech machines that help people access information and community literacy services was strong. In the early 1980s, the National Commission on Libraries and Information Science (NCLIS) sponsored a study of technology use and outcomes in literacy programs. It found that the software was not suitable for adult learning needs; it also found a lack of interest and anger among tutors, who felt they were being replaced by machines. When interviewed, however, adult learners said they enjoyed the privacy and flexibility the computers offered them (to drop in and use at any time). Most importantly, regardless of the software, adults were motivated to learn. This study influenced the direction of instructional technology in library literacy programs.[10]

By the mid-1980s, through funds from the Library Services and Construction Act (LSCA), state funds, and some private grants, programs in 11 states obtained computers. Many of these programs used computers in ways similar to nonliteracy services in libraries—for management purposes (to match learners with tutors), for instructional support (word processing), for supplemental instruction (commercial reading software), and as a primary means of instruction whereby students and tutors would use the software to read text. In Minneapolis, for example, staff reported that computers improved their programs by removing the stigma of limited literacy because adults had individual computers and most schools didn't.[11]

The largest library literacy computer project was in California. Staff felt that the computers attracted learners to the library but that the software didn't fit most adults' literacy needs. Generally, these projects did enforce self-directed learning activities, which benefited programs, as they often lacked tutors. Likewise, learners appreciated the computers' flexibility and step-by-step approach to learning. The computers appeared to be eventually accepted by tutors, especially after they received training. Yet among project leaders there was no agreement about the best software or hardware to purchase, how programs could collaborate with community agencies having computers, and how to share their resources.

It wasn't until the 1990s that private monies poured into library literacy programs. Through the Libraries in Literacy Across America initiative (a joint effort of the Wallace Foundation and the American Library Association), over a 6-year period millions of dollars went to 21 libraries to develop computer labs and facilities as well as other aspects of their programs. This fit with the national rhetoric of increasing access to computerized literacy learning in order to decrease the digital divide and the library rhetoric of technological innovation for equality of access. Yet an implicit economic agenda framed these efforts, that is, making adult literacy programs serve the labor market, as most grants went into technological development. This new labor market focus redefined literacy and played down the 1960s focus on poverty reduction. Consider how the American Library Association defined literacy:

> 21st Century Literacy is . . . [helping] children and adults develop skills they
> need to fully participate in an information society—whether it's learning to
> read or explore the Internet.[12]

The term "21st century literacy," drawn from then Vice President Al
Gore's agenda, emphasized information access and reducing the digital divide between rich and poor. What was neglected, however—something that
continues to be a problem—was how computers actually instruct and their
benefits for students' learning. The focus instead was on access and use.
Because many learners lacked access to personal computers at home, there
was little opportunity for learners to practice unless they came back to the
library. One-to-one instruction prevailed because it fit with the one-to-one
instruction of libraries and librarians' traditional dealings with individual
patrons. There has been virtually no criticism about the use of computers
in library literacy programs aside from occasional anecdotes. There were
many unanswered questions about the actual learning that occurred with
computers—they were indeed "oversold" to library literacy programs—but,
unlike in schools, they were not underused.

A CLOSER LOOK AT COMPUTER STUDIES
OF LIBRARY LITERACY PROGRAMS

There have been several major studies that reveal the diverse ways library
literacy programs used technology in the 1990s. In 1996, Gail Spangenberg
conducted a national survey of library literacy programs sponsored by the
Center for the Book. She surveyed 82 local library literacy programs in 32
states, as well as state literacy resource center directors and state librarians.
While her study investigated different areas within the library (e.g. the role
of the library, finance and funding, leadership, and state levels of support),
her focus on technology—its uses and limits—is revealing. She found that
almost all state librarians, library agency contacts, and local program directors supported heavier use of computers; more than four out of five favored
additional computer usage. Yet they also were cautious about its use; for example, only 44% of program directors said distance-learning technology should
be used more. One of the main reasons for this was because they were struggling financially to preserve their core literacy instruction services. They felt
that personal contact with tutors was something they wanted to preserve and
were concerned that more computers would disrupt this aspect of learning.

State resources also supported these efforts. In Oregon, LSCA grants
set up six learning stations in each public library and increased Internet connectivity. In Illinois, the state was committed to increasing training for technology, and in many other states, more effort was made to expand use of

the Internet. Local program staff saw computers as fitting into what they do, and, while they had plans to increase the number and use of computers, they felt constrained by funding—for training, hardware, software, more space, staffing, and, connectivity. The largest libraries in urban areas, like New York and Philadelphia, had the most ambitious technology plans, which they could clearly afford. Yet there was a lack of models for library literacy programs, since many were struggling with the same issues in computerizing their literacy programs. There was little knowledge about how other programs used it. Spangenberg concluded that more resources were needed in the planning effort.[13]

Another major study from 1997 to 1999 in Hilo, Hawai'i, examined the ways state and economic policies shaped computer use in library literacy programs by staff, tutors, and students. Hawai'i was one of the earlier technology adopters among library literacy programs in the country, and the program in Hilo was established as a model, with much money from state, national, and business communities pouring computers into the program.[14]

Taking a closer look at the history of Hawai'i's libraries and the influx of computers in Hawai'i is instructive. During the 1980s and 1990s, the Hawai'i State Public Library system downsized staff and print holdings (both books and magazines) while expanding building and audiovisual collections. With increasing automation, there were more computerized work processes and equipment, especially in the circulation department. The new state librarian appointed in 1982 by the State Board of Education, Bartholomew Kane, promoted a business model of librarianship with his "reengineering" plan and closer ties to the private sector. Library users were considered "customers." Librarians' positions were cut as new equipment, especially computers, was bought and book selection was outsourced in his campaign to create "libraries without walls." Public access computers were showcased and opened gates to establish a model library literacy program (in Hilo) with its computerized learning focus. Kane supported literacy programs, since they had potential for being privatized and included high-tech machines. He said that "literacy programs must include technology, media, math as well as reading. The focus should be on family literacy, using video, and computers to teach reading and writing."[15]

Directives to streamline and standardize services and staff statewide meant more part-time and temporary workers. The revamping of the catalog and circulation systems with automated systems brought additional controversies over contracts with companies. Funds for equipment and machines increased while monies for print holdings fell.

The major controversy in the state involved an outsourcing contract to a Maryland book distributor, signed by Kane, to select books and other materials without the consent of local librarians. Because of protests from Hawai'i librarians, the contract was dropped. Yet the brewing gender politics behind this issue was palpable, since a top White male administrator was trying to outsource the core job of many women librarians. The contract with Baker & Taylor (B&T) was canceled in 1996, and Kane left office in 1997. A new librarian, Virginia Lowell, was committed to restoring librarians' authority over selection of materials but not necessarily to funding more computer-based library literacy programs.[16]

The Computer-Assisted Learning Center (CALC) at the Hilo Public Library was a response to a number of different literacy forces emerging nationally and in the state in the early 1990s. Workplace literacy demands increased private funding, and technology grew nationally. This was reflected in Hilo, with over 50% of adults considered functionally illiterate and a high unemployment rate. Computers were viewed as part of the solution, and they were promoted in reports and grants. The connection of computers to new service industries and work for displaced agricultural workers was also explicit. When Bartholomew Kane was State Librarian, he linked literacy and the Hilo CALC library program to the business sector:

> One of the primary target groups of the Hilo CALC are the displaced agricultural workers of East Hawai'i County who now find it necessary to compete for jobs in other sectors. Many of these people believed that employment in the agricultural industry was for a lifetime and they never gave much credence to the necessity of learning those skills necessary to function in other jobs. This program has proved extremely successful in teaching many of these people the basic skills they require to qualify, apply, and compete for jobs in the open market.[17]

The belief that computers could help "retrain" workers came largely from top-level administrators. But it also fit the beliefs of librarians concerning lifelong learning, computer literacy, and self-education. Literacy programmers saw computers as part of socioeconomic mobility for adults who had trouble reading. Hilo community members saw CALC and the computers as a "free" education whereby library patron members could get no-cost personal computer training.

Hilo Public Library's literacy program began in 1991 as a "model." Although originally funding was through the Hawai'i state legislature and LSCA funds from 1992 through 1995, in subsequent years it was funded almost entirely by private foundations, businesses, and individual donations. Since Hawai'i Community College (HCC) dropped many of its remedial courses and Hilo Community School for Adults (HCSA) offered more night courses, CALC filled these gaps with one-on-one instruction, basic literacy, ESOL, and computer skills instruction in an unpressured atmosphere for learners. It also offered technology instruction (how to use computers and software) to library patrons. By 1999, with IBM grants and a small space in the back of the library, CALC had eight computers.

Coined by Maile Williams, a Hawaiian Young Adult librarian, who united Hawaiian beliefs about education and learning with library concepts of lifelong learning, the aperçu *A 'ohe pau ka 'ike i ka halau ho'okahi* (One can learn from many sources) defined CALC from its beginnings. She felt that the library needed to better serve local adults and young adults, especially Hawaiians in the community, by teaching computer and basic skills as well as reading instruction. The program was designed to assist tutors and then students, emphasizing self-education, in developing computer skills.

Rationales for computer use linked technology to the needs of the labor market. One report asked:

> If adult basic education skills were "computerized," could we affect more people more quickly at equal or lower cost? . . . Adults who learn basic skills on a computer also learn in the process about computers. The operational techniques absorbed as a by-product of instruction become in themselves marketable skills. These adults stand a better chance of competing for entry-level word processing jobs and job-training programs.[18]

CALC participants had to be age 12 or older and were called "patrons." The "patrons" were required to fill in a registration form and were given folders, which were used each time they came. The software on the computer included word-processing, assessment, and reading programs. Language arts, arithmetic, typing tutorials, and vocabulary programs were also available. These programs served functional literacy skill levels to grade 8. There was one printer.

Over the years, changes in curriculum occurred, with more emphasis on job training, math, and preparation for the General Education Development (GED) test. The number of personal computing (PC) students also increased, sometimes outnumbering the ESOL students. The PC students, advanced Adult Basic Education (ABE) students, and Job Training and Partnership Act (JTPA) students, plus one-time Internet instruction sessions increased student numbers by the end of 1997, with 1000+ hours of computer training being given. Staff paid special attention to those students who became volunteer tutors in an effort to give back to other adults what they had received.

That CALC changed from a modest place for tutors to "pass on" literacy to students to a center with eight computers, over 600 books, 20 volunteers, and 20 software programs, networking with other agencies and businesses and serving midlife students with an average age of 40, is notable. Such a shift is paradoxical, for with more computers came more computer students, fewer tutors, and more advanced students who could operate software programs without much assistance. ABE 1 and 2 students often left, while the more advanced students, especially the ones in a semester session at the local community college, remained.

For almost all of the ABE and ESOL students, as well as the computer students, little writing occurred with the available software. Sentence fill-ins represented "writing" as a formula. Instead, the students operated the computer-assisted programs by reading the questions, answering a set amount of possible questions, and then adding up their scores at the end to compare their "progress" to their last session. For ESOL students, there was little audio on the software, which they found limiting because they might not have known the sound of the word on the screen. When asked, most students could not remember the vocabulary they had just "learned," but they enjoyed getting a correct answer. Access to the Internet, including e-mail, was very limited.

How did the program fit into the library as it increasingly attracted more private funding and instructional technology? The head librarian supported it, as did other librarians, who felt positively about literacy programming but were conflicted as to whether or not it really fit well with primary library activities. One librarian expressed ambivalence about literacy work:

> How do we take on another service when we can barely provide adequate materials and services of core library functions? It seems idealistic and wonderful for libraries to get more involved with literacy and lifelong learning. But it does not seem realistic. I'd like to see libraries provide excellent core services rather than provide a wide array of mediocre service.

Other librarians believed in the importance of literacy and wanted to help and learn more about it, but they saw the goals and purposes of literacy programs and libraries as divergent. Literacy programs were viewed as more self-sufficient and had a strong business orientation, whereas the library staff were more *o'hana* (family) oriented.[19]

Computers at CALC served multiple purposes and changed over a period of one year, 1997–1998. New machines arrived, and new software programs and equipment—like printers, a scanner, and voice software—were installed. Sometimes they substituted for tutoring and sometimes they supplemented tutoring sessions. Most importantly, they contributed to a skills-based approach at the heart of CALC. The new technology also fit with a library philosophy of self-education and independent learning.

The computers took center stage for many reasons. They were used for publicity, symbolizing the new economic changes that could move the Big Island from its agricultural base to a service labor market; they were also viewed as reflections of the modern automated public library. As more computers arrived, pressure grew to provide library users with access to them. Since the library lacked formalized basic computer skills instruction, CALC introduced library patrons to computers and the Internet. CALC computers were important for attracting matching grants from companies geared toward high technology and for educating highly literate students, but they could not promise jobs. As learning tools, they were especially problematic because of software limitations. Often computer programs were responsible for moving students through CALC, inspiring them to fulfill their possibilities, yet propelling them out of CALC because they were boring. Computerized assessments were supposed to determine how much and how well CALC students had learned. These assessments were given to students upon intake and every 6 months thereafter to determine their movement through the program.

This study, using ethnographic methods, concluded that the symbolic value of the computers as part of accumulating human capital for access to the labor market and higher social status diminished because of the programs' low-grade functions, the lack of teacher instruction, few jobs in the community to work in with computers, and the decontextualized content. After all, it was "computer-assisted" and focused on skills. The computers offered privacy, but they were isolating. They offered students a sense of control for performing basic operations but not for manipulating computers for their own purposes. Given these limitations, the Internet offered the most possibilities for learner creativity and control (flexibility and modification of features), and it was social. Yet it had very limited use, and it was hard to gauge whether or not it was an effective learning tool.[20]

The next major study on library literacy programs was conducted in 2000 by Leigh Estabrook and Edward Lakner and was sponsored by the Library Research Center and the University of Illinois with funding from the Wallace Fund. Researchers surveyed 1,067 libraries (out of 1,500 that were targeted) asking about a range of library services. They found that that 90% provided literacy services in terms of developing collections (80%), partnering with other literacy programs through space and referring patrons (90%), and offering direct literacy instruction (30%). With direct instruction, the larger the library (more funds, full-time staff), the more involvement in literacy programming. Of those that didn't provide direct instruction, most (74%) were in communities that already provided such instruction through other agencies. Only 8% of librarians did not provide these services because they felt that literacy programs were not within the mission of the library. Still, funding by states and local communities seemed to play a large role here, as other studies have shown. Estabrook and Lakner showed that libraries' annual investment in adult literacy correlated to the size of their service area and that local taxes supplied most of literacy activities (from the library's operating budget), followed by state aid, private donations, gifts, and federal grants.[21]

Most direct instruction programs had a full range of activities and served ABE, ESOL, and family literacy populations, many in collaboration with other providers in their communities. Although there was no statistical correlation, as shown in previous library literacy studies, leadership and size appeared to be important variables in supporting literacy programming. Over 60% of directors serving libraries of over half a million people gave a "very high" to "high" priority to literacy services compared to those serving less than 50,000. Estabrook and Lakner concluded that libraries spent $26–36 million dollars a year on literacy programs and served 43,000 adult basic education learners, 31,000 ESOL learners, and 20,000 family literacy learners. They considered libraries to be a "major player in the provision of literacy programs and services for adults."[22]

Of the types of teaching, one-to-one instruction was more often used for ABE students, with one-third using only this method. Computer-assisted instruction was reported in over 70% of the ABE programs, and 60% of ESOL programs. They used it for writing (36%); the Internet, CD-ROMs, and online services (33%); as well as e-mail (16%). Most programs, however, used books much more than computers, with over 80% using commercial textbooks and 60% using actual work and community materials.

The programs were open-entry and -exit and used little testing; while there was formal enrollment, there was little formalized assessment of literacy skills. As a result, most learners spent little actual time in the programs, with 9% receiving over 150 hours of instruction and about a quarter receiving 100 hours of instruction. While many learners persisted in these programs, most dropped out. Librarians felt that learners did not persist because of lack of personal motivation, with child care as a major problem, rather than insufficient instruction. Few of the programs provided support services; 28% provided some type of child care, and 18% offered transportation of some type. Respondents reported that libraries networked with other agencies and advertised their services. Most of these computer-based literacy programs had waiting lists of students wanting to get in.[23]

While this study was important for gathering basic statistics on the types of current literacy services that were being provided, there was little analysis about why this occurred. Serious questions about financially supporting programs when student persistence was very low arise. How can attrition be reduced? What types and how much technology is needed to support such efforts?

In collaboration with the ALA, the Wallace Foundation (formerly called the DeWitt-Wallace Readers Digest Fund) invested $4 million in the mid-1990s to fund a major study of model library literacy programs to answer these and other questions. The Wallace Foundation regarded libraries as important players in adult literacy but saw them as constrained by lack of resources and technical services and support.[24] Relying on the results of the Spangenberg study, as well as national adult literacy studies, the foundation sought to improve programs. In 1996, 13 adult literacy programs in Florida, Kentucky, Louisiana, Maryland, and Ohio received planning grants to improve their core services—curriculum, instruction, technology, and assessment. The libraries spent half of their funds on technology and the other half on referrals, information, and instructional developments. Access to computers was important, and so the programs increased wiring, software, and hardware because they wanted to provide learners with choices. They used computers to diversify instruction, spice up curriculum, and help assess literacy skills. The next step for these programs was to apply for implementation grants.[25]

The Persistence Study

In 1999, after the Spangenberg and Estabrook and Lakner studies revealed a national picture of library literacy programs, showing that they needed greater resources for technology, the Wallace Foundation invited libraries that had received planning grants to apply for implementation grants. Five libraries won. Since these libraries had received the initial round of planning grants, they had already learned some important lessons about recruiting learners, training tutors, and creating materials. They were highlighted in the Wallace Foundation reports as being able to increase and integrate instruction. Could they help students to stay in programs and become fully literate?

Successful grantees did research on students to learn their needs and barriers (focus groups, for example); they implemented tutor training models and changed instructional methods; they extended hours, staying open more days and nights, and, most importantly, brought in more computers and developed sophisticated labs. The programs received thousands of dollars in technical support to help them with all of the above. The purpose of these diverse strategies was to widen and intensify participation of learners, as major federal studies had indicated that dropout levels, especially for those with low literacy levels, were especially high. Access, participation, and persistence (students staying in programs) were of great interest.

As we will see, computer use, apart from Internet use, remained more as a strategy to increase access to the program than as a learning tool. For example, one library's rationale for computer use was that other community literacy providers could afford teachers but not hardware, software, and construction of websites, all of which the library had.[26] Computers seemed like a magic bullet because they helped programs recruit more students. They also allowed the programs to offer more instruction, intensifying participation through hourly usage rates. Yet little monitoring of students' learning from computers occurred. This was a criticism made by one of the managers of the program, who questioned why so many computers were bought with little research on how they improved instruction. Were they oversold to students? What uses did they have?[27]

These and other questions were asked in relation to persistence by two research teams, beginning in 1999. They studied five libraries and ten computer-based literacy programs at the Queens Borough Public Library's three Adult Learning Centers (Jamaica, Rochdale, Flushing) in New York; the New York Public Library's Centers for Reading and Writing (Fordham, Wakefield, and Seward Park); the Greensboro Public Library's Chavis and Glenwood branches in North Carolina; Redwood City Public Library's Project READ in California; and the Oakland Public Library's Second Start in California. The research was a collaborative project consisting of a team from MDRC (formerly known as the Manpower Demonstration Research Corporation), which did the quantitative data collection, and a team from the National Center for the Study of Adult Learning and Literacy (NCSALL), a federally funded agency based at Harvard University, which collected qualitative data. Together they examined the ways the programs implemented these strategies and their effects on students, particularly rates of participation in the programs.

These programs were selected because they were considered exemplary models located in different geographic areas that had intentionally recruited learners with low levels of literacy and language skills who had been barred from entering community colleges because they had failed their placement tests and/or did not reveal documentation of citizenship. In fact most, if not all, of the programs contained many new immigrant groups who turned out to be heavy computer users.

Computers were brought into the programs not just for instructional learning purposes, but for research and administrative purposes. MDRC needed numbers on students' demographic traits, rates of enrollment, hourly instructional usage, the types of instructional modes used, and their monthly retention in a program over time, from the beginning to the end of the study. They also needed to test the students and would map their scores to their literacy skill and participation levels.

The NCSALL qualitative team was interested in how computers were used in programs. Researchers observed student use of labs between 1999 and 2003 and interviewed students, staff and tutors, as well as nearby community agency staff. Program reports and students' academic records were also examined.

Unsurprisingly, the most popular technology in the library literacy programs was computers. But there were also audio books, photocopiers, CDs, and TVs. Computers were set up in labs or in corners that allowed staff to oversee and help students. The machines were often accompanied by printers, scanners, and headsets.

After signing in, students usually entered a password or registered before they sat down for 50-minute to 1-hour periods. The commercial software featured both phonics and creative writing, diagnostic and simulated tests (from the Test of English as a Foreign Language [TOEFL] to driving programs), and web access. All labs were staffed by Americorps interns, paid staff, and high school and college computer mavens who often set up groups of students on the same programs and gave individualized help on an as-needed basis. The most popular programs for ESOL were Rosetta Stone and English Discoveries, with students often writing words on their steno pads and looking them up in their electronic or print dictionaries. In using the programs, students often used headsets but less so their microphones. TOEFL test preparation, software typing tutors, the Internet, and word processing (for higher-level students) were also popular with ESOL students. Literacy students used a wider range of commercial software, especially phonics programs (Ultimate Phonics, Phonics Alive, Reading SOS, Earobics), creative writing programs (Write Out Loud) and specialty software (such as typing tutors and spelling programs). As an appealing instructional medium, the computers accounted for more hourly instruction. Here is what some programs did with their computer labs between 1999 and 2003.[28]

New York Public Library's Centers for Reading and Writing

Due to the heavy emphasis on providing access to literacy instruction for New York's least literate populations and the constant lack of tutors, computers seemed to fill a necessary gap; with more resources than most literacy programs, the Centers for Reading and Writing could provide many different types of software and hardware. In addition, the Centers had a literary reputation—with students as authors, so there were more creative uses of the computers. The program implemented mentoring systems whereby college students assisted ESOL students and others to navigate software programs. As more web-based ESOL programs started to appear, the mentors and students would use these together. Tutors often used computers to edit and transfer the students' writings into a typeface for many self-published booklets. E-mail classes were also set up. In a 2003 cost survey, the director rated computer labs as having a positive impact on the persistence of students and felt the staff time, dollar amount, and equipment were worth it and that the program would be continued.

Oakland Public Library's Second Start

Second Start served many African Americans and increasing numbers of immigrants. The program provided an alternative education for those at very low levels of literacy who were unserved by local community colleges. Staff encouraged one-to-one tutoring, using small groups in the computer lab, where full-time and part-time staff worked with many different types of students, some of whom were classified as learning disabled. While the tutoring was heavily phonics-based (they used Laubach books), the computer software was diverse (including pre-phonics software, such as Earobics) and offered students opportunities to write stories and to test and practice their grammar and word knowledge skills. With staff assisting students, the Internet became available. The upscale computer lab, which was a capstone to the program, had moved from an open to a closed space where students could concentrate better. It also extended its hours so that more students could use it. Gradually, staff trained tutors to integrate the computers into their instruction; over time, computer instruction seemed to became a normal part of instruction. Computer staff spent about 3 weeks integrating students into the lab and then weaned them for individual use. Staff then might intervene and help students on the spot by using a new computer tracking system that monitored each student's use and by observing them. New students were often in the lab as they waited for tutors, who were in short supply. Computers served as substitute tutors in these cases. Students used phonics programs more often than the more labor-intensive creative writing programs, particularly those who would be considered learning disabled.

Due to its location in the San Francisco Bay area and aggressive grant seeking, Second Start staff were able to capture many grants for its computer lab; one major computer company donated money for learning disabilities resources. Staff also made the computer lab accessible to deaf students and those with cerebral palsy. Staff interviews revealed that the computer lab absorbed much staff time and equipment, yet they were sometimes unsure of its impact on students remaining in the program, since they noticed that the students used it unpredictably, even when hours were extended. Because of the software, however, which had improved over the years, they felt their computer lab was worth the effort. They believed the tutors were more enthusiastic about the lab once they received training, and the students were receiving more diverse instruction.

Greensboro Public Library's Glenwood Branch

The Glenwood branch library had responded to its immigrant communities by providing multicultural collections, computer labs, one-on-one and small-group tutoring, and an array of other cultural programming through collaborative enterprises with local organizations. The program served as a center for cultural exchange between its immigrant newcomers (from East Africa, Southeast Asia, and Hispanic/Latino) and native-born Southerners. Examples would be its conversation groups in English and Spanish, citizenship classes, and women's literacy classes as well as its nonprofit center that focused on community renewal and partnerships with local agencies. The computer lab, housed in a small closetlike space near the entrance of the library, had updated ESOL software and hardware. It was staffed by multilingual Americorp volunteers who assisted students with their questions and made them feel at home. They advised lab users about what software to use based on staff diagnosis of their learning levels. Advanced ESOL students used an English Language Instruction System (ELLIS) and TOEFL programs, and those with lower levels used Rosetta Stone. These students could rotate through the collections, classes, conversation and small groups, and then attend the lab. Staff viewed the lab as a complement to self-study and appropriate for independent users. ESOL students appeared comfortable in the lab.

The program established staggered hours of operation to accommodate its many shift workers in factories and restaurants with slots in the afternoon, morning, and evening. Most of the time the lab was crowded. Access to the lab was important, as the library only had four main computers in the main room. The director felt that the amount of staff time devoted to purchasing and maintaining new computers impacted the persistence of students and was worth the effort.

These program descriptions and analyses, drawn from the larger Porter, Cuban, and Comings study demonstrate clearly in this secondary analysis that the computers were largely an operational strategy to give students increased access to technology and intensify their participation. It served more as a "use technology" than it did as an instructional technology. It was relevant in the following main ways to all of the programs:

- It increased hourly usage of the programs without the need to staff the lab intensively with full-time employees. Computer labs also increased the student population because computers allowed for waiting-list reductions and the induction of more students without tutors.
- Computers served as substitute tutors. Computers become a fill-in when tutors left until new ones were found, or when a new student entered a program and could not immediately be matched to a tutor.
- The lab offset the other instructional modes (one-to-one tutoring, small groups, classes) and provided self-study options. The labs had the effect of diversifying the instruction and providing incentives for students, once they got the hang of working alone, to use another form of instruction.
- The computer labs and the software helped to diversify the library literacy program populations, drawing in varied students. Students who were ESOL, learning disabled, or atypical (could not be placed with tutors) used the computer lab extensively.
- Computer labs increased the multimedia collection—one program spent $40,000 on software. Computers gradually dominated technology acquisition, overshadowing other forms in programs, including television and audio books.

These points, based on direct observation and staff interviews, empha-size the uses of computers and computer labs by programs. But what about the students' learning? The focus in library literacy programs was almost entirely on access, on use, and as an instructional mode for ensuring par-ticipation, rather than as a reflective learning technology. No program systematically monitored student learning from using the computers or as-sessed the effects of computer use on them, although programs did assess their general learning. While many programs tried to integrate the comput-ers into other aspects of instruction, even training tutors and institutional-izing the labs within the overall library, the labs were often physically and ideologically separate from the rest of the program. Unlike schools that focus on instruction and learning in ways that may restrict computer use, these literacy-based programs made computers available to students but without first learning the students' specific computer-related learning needs or using their learning on the computers to intensively develop their inter-ests, knowledge, and competencies. Yet the computers were not underused. Let's look more closely at some themes that emerged from studies of these diverse programs.[29]

THEMES OF TECHNOLOGY LEARNING FOR STUDENTS

Acquiring Basic Skills and Knowledge

Students gained access to the computers and did more than simply "use" them. They did gain some skills and knowledge. The students' uses of the computers was essentially nonreflective, focused on low-level skills and knowledge. In other words, the use was "instructivist" rather than "constructivist." The instructivist approach focuses on using software in standard ways—students following onscreen directions, answering questions, and filling in blanks. Constructivist approaches focus on using software programs that engage students to deepen their understanding of concepts through writing and project-based learning. The library literacy programs tended to support the first type.[30] Program staff were adept at teaching learning strategies, espe-cially orientation strategies (i.e., gaining comfort from using the computers), but not management (giving autonomy to students), information processing (i.e., cognitive strategies to gain knowledge), and evaluation of outcomes (i.e., allowing students to self-assess and regulate their learning).[31] Literacy was indeed learned as students gained more than just hands-on skills, but they seldom gained a deeper understanding of the ways of learning and problem solving.[32] Simple use of technology, even the Internet, did not reinforce higher-level thinking skills or metacognitive skills, and while information literacy was developed among students in their more informal learning, this tended to be at a lower level of problem solving. From the students' viewpoint however, the distinctions were less clear. The students believed the computers were crucial for obtaining jobs.

Computer Skills Opening Doors

Most students believed that computers opened doors to mainstream society. Not using the machines made them feel like they were outsiders. One student confessed: "You have to learn to use a computer. The most [important] thing here now is [the] computer, so you have to learn to use [the] computer; you have to learn something else. . . . You have to look to another source." Students who did not receive help in instructional technology often labeled themselves as "dinosaurs" or, as one student said, "a computer illiterate." Students whose jobs were becoming automated were even more sold on computers as the wave of the future. One student who worked as an airport mechanic commented:

> Everything I do involve computers. I have a friend, right—some friends become like family to me. He ask me things on the computer. But at the same time I only know a little about it. . . . So, ultimately more people on a computer, because a computer is all it asks, is to learn more.[33]

Computers were also equated with acquiring Standard English vocabulary and general knowledge. One student, when asked whether she preferred one-to-one conversation or computers, said it was the latter because she could learn grammar: "Computer, I learn a lot of words. I said—even I cannot spelling right away, but I can read it from the computer."

Most of the students did not have computers at home and used library computers for themselves and their children. Of those who did have computers at home, most of whom were ESOL students, the machines were either broken or were used exclusively by the children. Still, they viewed computers as important for their children's futures, if not their own. One Salvadoran single mother did not have a computer at home and brought her children to the library to use them. She felt it worked for them, but not for herself, and understood that it was heavily valued. She said:

> Actually, I don't know about much in computer. I just know the basic. Well, I'm not really kind of a computer person. Not really. She [her tutor] always says, you know, "it's always good to know" and things.

Learning to Use Technology

Basic technology learning was important in the programs. According to Lynda Ginsburg, there are several different forms of technology learning. The main ones could be characterized as technology as curriculum (gaining technology skills), technology as a complement to instruction (commercial educational software), and technology as instruction (using technology to solve problems, as in doing Internet searches).[34] The library literacy programs emphasized the first two forms, as a way to give low-level learners access to computers and prepare them for more educational study. Since many learners in the program did not initially know how to use the computers and would be considered at very low levels of English-language literacy, the first type of instruction they received was getting familiar with the keyboard and machine operation.

Students who had never before used a computer were often intimidated and depended on staff or tutors to help them. When asked about her computer experience, one student explained the process in concrete terms: "The keys. You put your finger in it, and you press, and a light come on, which it is S, or A, or D, or K, which you press, and it on the screen." She described the experience more fully:

> He [tutor] have the class going on with the computer people, and then he said, "B., if you interested in the computer." I said, I never, never go on that. I am so nervous, my skin trembling, my hands sweating. Yes. I tell him I never put my hands on a typewriter or a computer. And he said, you will learn, B., you will learn. And he encouraged me, and he take me to the computer. I was so nervous, and I was trembling. And he said, you will learn, and my hands shaking on the keys.

Eventually she worked on the computers before and after her sessions, coming to the program an hour before tutoring to practice typing. She, like many other students, slowly built her sense of self-efficacy about doing computer tasks. Students often said they enjoyed computers for the typing: "Yes, I love it," one student said, "you know, because I like to type, typing, and a lesson." Another student liked that he could change the typeface so that he could see what he was writing, and added, "Oh, I come here and I go in the computer room, and I read, type out loud. I hear the words and everything, I'll be in there typing."

Some tutors asked students to use the computer as a way to reinforce and extend writing assignments from their small groups. In these cases, students often wrote their assignment with a pencil and paper and then, after it was edited with the help of the tutor, it was inputted into a computer. In other cases, students used the computer to compose a piece of writing, although this was observed on rare occasions and mostly as e-mail. Students also used the educational software to practice skills such as decoding and to acquire vocabulary. Well-trained staff might use it to complement instruction. One said, "When appropriate, it seems to make sense to combine both traditional hands-on reading and writing with activities in the computer lab. There are cases when the groundwork has to be laid to make the computer learning make sense."

Due to the learner-centered approaches of the programs, the students had many choices about using the computers. While some students flat out refused to use a computer, others used it as a supplement and preparatory tool. Students felt that the computers would always be there for them to use, and they decided on the right time to use them. The learners could use computers at any point in the process—while waiting for tutors and between tutoring or class sessions. The computers were especially important for ESOL students who were on waiting lists for classes in their communities or were already enrolled in large performance-based types of classes. They used the computers to reinforce and practice their listening, comprehension, and vocabulary skills.

The computer labs were open for longer periods of time than the time involved in tutoring sessions or classes. Students could drop into labs during the day, the evening, or on the weekends. Most computer use could be completed within an hour; if they needed more time, they could make an appointment or sign in. When programs extended their evening hours, they often did so with computer lab time. Computer lab hours were easier to manipulate because of the mostly part-time staff that ran the labs and the late and weekend hours of the library. Due to the staff and tutor shortages, computer labs were heavily promoted by the programs, along with other self-directed learning activities, including book use and borrowing tapes and books from the in-house and host libraries. For students who were self-starters, it worked well. One student explained:

> Well, we don't get a tutor. So, we can't wait all of our life on the tutor. We have to help ourself and each other with other students, you could help yourself. You don't have to depend on the tutor. You have tape there; you have the computer there.

Internet Use Reinforcing Information Literacy

This aspect was the closest to imaginative uses of the computer. However, while information was obtained creatively, the learning that occurred was unclear. The information students were often looking for was on the Internet, and it was mainly for recreational and communication purposes. One student said:

> I like using the computer. . . . I like watching wrestling. So I go and
> look at stuff on the Internet. I type. I do e-mail. . . . I didn't know
> nothing when I came here. . . . I didn't know how to use the com-
> puter or nothing. . . . That's the only time that I use it, when I am
> here. . . . I have been sending [e-mails] like to a few of my tutors that
> I had, two tutors that left from here.

Another student interacted online with a TV studio representative about
a popular television show. One program had an Internet class that taught
students how to search for information on various topics. One class focused
on travel, and students found out how to be smart consumers in selecting hotels
and airfares. Another class focused on e-mails (setting them up, writing them,
etc.). Yet information on jobs and housing, as well as other nonrecreational
issues, was also obtained via the Internet, especially when staff members
helped students who brought in interests and materials from their outside
lives.

Helping students use the Internet could be the most effective for insti-
gating reflective or constructivist instruction. Its use could improve instruction through added practice or the development of new skills and knowledge,
not just practice, repetition, and reinforcement of instruction—as with so
much "instructivist" software.

The Need for Professional Staff

Students needed knowledgeable, trained staff to help them initially use the
computers and for sustained learning. Using the Internet and commercial
software required staff help. Yet the staff in the lab were often part-timers,
high school students, and college interns. Rarely were they full-time professionals. The designated staff would help students put in CD-ROMs and exit
computer programs, as well as restart computers when they froze. But they
did not fully assess students' learning in the lab or know if they were learning
at all, except in a few cases where full-time staff and college mentors were
assigned to a lab. Therefore, it was never clear as to what instructional mode
could be attributed to a student's success or lack of progress. Observations of
the programs showed that many students needed constant ongoing instructional assistance on the computers. But staff assistance was not always available.

Another problem was that the computer hardware, headsets, and printers
would often break down due to the constant use and the large amount of
memory required of new software. Part-time staff could not solve this problem. Lack of technical assistance was a pervasive problem in nearly all programs. Libraries did have technical maintenance staff, but the department
was often located elsewhere and would often take a long time to fix the problem. Only in the California programs was assistance available due to many

of the volunteers, staff, and tutors working in the computer industry. Installing new computers and new software could take a long time with few technical maintenance people available, in addition to the red tape that exacerbated the problem. Because libraries were highly bureaucratic systems, this added to the time conflict and caused misunderstandings between literacy and library staff. Despite the promotion of these programs by the top leadership in libraries, a constant source of tension was the lack of communication between the literacy staff and core library staff in other departments, including technical maintenance, who didn't understand the purpose of the programs.

Other problems involving staff emerged. Self-study, for example, was often difficult in the labs. Sometimes the labs were crowded and noisy. Students would yell questions across the room to staff, distracting other students. Moreover, not all staff were sold on computers as a primary learning technology in their programs and worried when they saw students overusing some software programs—repeating lessons and not challenging themselves intellectually. Some tutors felt that technology replaced them and prevented them from interacting and developing relationships with students.

Some commercial software did not allow for learners to adjust learning as a teacher might do based on students' progress. Using computers as dummy tutors, therefore, was not conducive to reflective learning. Moreover, there was less monitoring, evaluating, and seeing patterns of use and building on them, despite attempts by the programs to introduce more sophisticated learning assessments. Even more advanced students, as they graduated to more sophisticated programs, needed additional support to scaffold their learning to higher stages. These later stages of help and teaching were neglected in a program with few staff. Even when students were perceived as having mastered so many software programs and appeared confident, even at ease with the computer, their more advanced intellectual needs may have been overlooked or not attended to as their computer skills developed.

LESSONS LEARNED

From these illustrations, it is clear that computers were favored in these programs and that most students used them as part of the "free learning" of libraries. However, it is unclear that computers actually helped students learn very much as an "instructional" technology if low levels of learning were observed and learning on computers was not monitored. Staff helped students to orient themselves around the computers, and more learning choices were offered to them. Still, computers were used primarily as "tools first." Access does not guarantee use; use does not guarantee desired learning.[35] Part of this problem is simply that although computers change the landscape of literacy programs, technology may not necessarily be considered as a part of the library program philosophy.[36] This would include how the computer lab fit into the rest of their program and its mission, as well as beliefs about computers as an effective learning mode. These issues need to be factored into a library environment that is saturated with computers but not necessarily with learning.

The Brooklyn Public Library staff, for example, questioned the low-level learning they saw students engaged in and began to focus on computers to support writing, project-based learning, and as part of a new model of tutor training and building staff development. They also focused on technology support measured by change in hourly usage and started to view the library more as a "learning place."[37]

Since the learning in the computer labs in the persistence study was observed to be unsystematic and poorly integrated into the rest of the program instruction, it remained simplistic, and there was a question as to whether or not it could promote reflective or constructivist types of learning—or even effective learning and motivation.[38]

The success of library literacy programs in acquiring technology among adult basic education agencies in communities has been unquestioned. Yet the success of making technology available in these programs—based on vendor promises or simple hope—rather than any clear evidence that it increases literacy learning among students became evident in time. Moreover, a lack of an instructional infrastructure, staff training, curriculum integration, and standards undermined the usefulness of these new technologies as a teaching and learning tool. The heaviest focus was on moving computers into library space, along with attracting new students and patrons and offering them something "different." This pragmatic focus was part of the larger library strategy for introducing computers. Computer labs became part of the existing institutional structure and part of the transformation of libraries. Not so for schools.

The next chapter focuses on instructional technology in schools and why computers were so slow to take hold in comparison to libraries and their literacy programs even though both institutions adopted business models. Group instruction of students prevailed, and it was far harder to bring the new technologies into schools.[39]

CHAPTER 4

Technology in Public Schools

Libraries have changed dramatically in the past half-century in using new technologies to give individual patrons full access to collections and advance literacy. Bar codes, automated book circulation, and fast Internet access to materials speed library patrons to the sources they want. Most public libraries in big cities have adult literacy programs with extensive use of computers and tutors, mirroring other library activities, where one-on-one instruction is prized.

Schools, however, have been less spectacular in their changes and far slower to apply new technologies to teaching and learning. They have also done it differently. In schools, much of the daily work to advance literacy and achieve the many other goals of tax-supported schooling remain unautomated and seemingly resistant to ubiquitous use of new technologies. Much of this is related to the school structure, pedagogical issues, and the aims of education as varied stakeholders interpret them. The past and present story of access to and use of technology in schools may help readers understand these notable differences.

ACCESS TO AND USE OF TECHNOLOGY
IN PUBLIC SCHOOLS

School administrators, parents, and teachers introduced personal computers into classroom instruction in the late 1970s, but the automating of administrative tasks for purchasing, personnel records, and gathering student data began in the 1960s. Now, more than two decades after the introduction of the desktop computer to public schools, the nation's schools—both rural and urban, wealthy and poor—are only coming close to providing students full access (largely achieved for teachers) to a powerful tool for teaching and learning. From 125 students per computer in 1984 to just under

5 students per computer in 2003—with many districts already close to a 1:1 ratio in 2007—computers in schools are everywhere.[1]

The embrace of information and communication technologies (ICT) in schools by policymakers, parents, business and civic leaders, and many educators in the past quarter-century is similar in some respects to earlier responses to new technologies that promised increased teacher and student productivity in classrooms. Before there were computers, school policymakers had introduced film and radio in the 1920s and instructional television in the 1950s as technological innovations to make teaching and learning faster and better. The introduction of these older technologies resembles the later introduction of computers in several ways:

1. Policymakers, not teachers, made the decisions to buy and deploy film projectors, radios, and television.
2. In each case there was initial excitement among efficiency-minded policymakers and administrators over how the technological innovation would revolutionize teaching and learning. Equipment was purchased and put into schools (e.g., a few film projectors for each elementary school and one for each department in a high school; a radio in every classroom; television monitors in school libraries or on carts) for teachers to use; then researchers went into schools to see how often and in which ways teachers were using these technologies in lessons. These academic studies often showed very limited use by teachers. Finally, disillusionment among policymakers spread and teachers were condemned for being resistant to technology.[2]

But ICT is vastly different from film, radio, and television as a tool for teaching and learning. First, earlier technologies were sparingly distributed among schools, and teachers had to compete for limited film inventories or rigidly scheduled times for radio and, later, television programs. Second, these technologies came from the entertainment industry, and students listened and watched passively; films and TV had the gloss of something that was fun, not educational.

Because of these significant differences between these earlier technological innovations and computers, comparing them is like comparing horse-drawn trolleys and bullet trains: They are both means of transportation but hugely different in their effects on passengers. So it comes as little surprise that, as these potent machines become available to every student, their champions paint utopian pictures of transformed teaching and learning unlike anything that existed before. In these hypothetical scenarios, students work alone or in small groups using laptops or small, handheld wireless devices. In school and at home, their use is almost entirely individualized, and teachers act as coaches to strengthen independent learning. Literacy is transferred smoothly and swiftly through these new technologies.[3]

Based on the history of schools adopting and using earlier technological innovations, however, we question these rose-tinted edutopias where learning is 24/7 and highly individualized. We question these scenarios because technology reformers persistently ignore the multiple roles schools and teachers perform in this society (e.g., character building), the purpose of schools in a democracy (as a public good, not a private one), the resilient structures and processes of schools (e.g., the age-graded school with self-contained classrooms and separate chunks of curriculum assigned to each grade), and, most important, what has happened in schools over the past century when such dreams have been launched again and again as well-intended improvements (e.g., educational television). Finally, we question these scenarios because of the two-decade long experience of wiring schools, buying hardware and software, and reducing the ratio of students to computers to below five per machine and the disappointing results—to promoters —of technology use in classrooms.

Even when 1:1 ratios have been reached in some school districts and have become widespread in higher education, the lack of substantial evidence for their regular use in classrooms, or for increased learning, raises doubts about schools as computerutopias. Moreover, these doubts lead to questions about the attempts by technology companies not only to fill schools with laptops and software geared, supposedly, to raising test scores but also to sell computerlike toys and other paraphernalia to toddlers. Why, then, have schools received so much attention regarding computers for instruction?

Before looking at the experiences of the past two decades of ICT in K–12, we need to make clear the dominant reasons given by policymakers, vendors, and business and civic leaders who press school districts to adopt ICT and teachers and students to use computers in their classrooms to satisfy elite-driven social reforms that turn education into a cure-all.

WHY HAVE COMPUTERS IN SCHOOLS?

What reasons do campaigners for ICT offer to persuade U.S. presidents, state governors, legislators at all levels, school board members, and parents to invest in ICT to the extent of ensuring that each student has a computer in school? Over the past two decades, three reasons have turned up again and again in the words, arguments, and handouts policymakers, business and civic leaders, and parents have used to persuade skeptics to adopt ICT. We begin with a composite quote drawn from liberal and conservative elected officials in the United States during the late 1990s that summed up the current wisdom.

We are entering the Information Age—a time of change equivalent to the shift from the Agricultural to the Industrial Age. The resulting deregulated global economy is bringing freedom and democracy to the rest of the world, and technological wonders to America. But if you want to enjoy it, you have to compete against six billion people out there, most of whom will work for a lot less than you will. The price of labor is set in South China. If you want to live seven times better, you have to be seven times more efficient. You should get all the technical training you can get, pack a computer on your back, and get out there and compete.[4]

Trumpeting this message throughout the media, pundits like Thomas Friedman see the future of the United States as determined by new technologies, "Why all this ed-anxiety today?" Friedman asks. He answers: "Because computers, fiber-optic cable, and the Internet have leveled the economic playing field, creating a global platform that more workers anywhere can now plug into and play on."[5]

As for schools, Louis Gerstner Jr., IBM's chief executive officer, minced few words about the task facing American schools:

Before we can get the education revolution rolling, we need to recognize that our public schools are low-tech institutions in a high-tech society. The same changes that have brought cataclysmic change to every facet of business can improve the way we teach students and teachers. And it can also improve the efficiency and effectiveness of how we run our schools.[6]

And in the last decade, there has been a surge of states and districts buying laptops to achieve a 1:1 ratio of student to computer. The argument for each student having a laptop uses a familiar claim that computers are neutral tools making all technologies equal. It goes like this: Each student has a textbook, each student has a pen and notebook, and each student should have a computer. In what business, in what hospital, in what police precinct, in what university—laptop champions ask—do four or five employees, doctors, officers, or professors have to compete for one computer? If you want literate and productive workers, give each one a computer or handheld device.[7]

The sentiments behind these words about global economics and the impact on the U.S. workplace and schooling helped fuel the astonishing outpouring of federal, state, and private monies over the past decade in wiring schools, accessing the Internet, buying millions of computers and software programs, and funding staff development to get teachers to use these machines in their daily classroom routines.

Other reasons rivaled the potent economic rationale for advancing literacy and providing technical skills for youth competing in an ever-changing labor market in a knowledge-based economy. Advocates claimed that ICT would also make teaching and learning more productive—much more would be taught and learned in less time; moreover, learning would be better, that is, students would be active, engaged, and focused on real-world tasks. Students would work together on projects that would require inquiry, collection of data, and analysis, and then present their work to peers and the community. As one report put it, "The real promise of technology in education lies in its potential to facilitate fundamental, qualitative changes in the nature of teaching and learning."[8]

At a 1996 national educational summit held at the corporate headquarters of IBM, governors, corporate leaders, top federal officials, and a sprinkling of educators heard President Clinton address the group on the importance of academic standards, tests, and technology. The final official statement from the summit wrapped the three divergent purposes holding together the ad hoc reform coalition into one sentence:

> We are convinced that technology, if applied thoughtfully and well integrated into a curriculum, can be utilized as a helpful tool to assist student learning, provide access to valuable information, and ensure a competitive edge for our workforce.[9]

Finally, there is the social justice argument that if all students, regardless of their family income, had access to ICT, then they would have access to jobs in an ever-changing labor market dependent on knowledge-based occupations. Deep concerns over a digital divide separating rich from poor, urban from suburban, have turned companies and school districts to ensuring that all children have access to new technologies.[10]

Taken together, these reasons still provide a powerful rationale for districts to buy wireless networks, laptops, and software. Because of the huge investments of school districts in ICT over the past two decades, inspecting what has occurred in classrooms becomes a necessary task and indicates the ways in which technological problems have replaced and redefined more entrenched sociopolitical issues in society.[11]

The presence of new technologies in classrooms tells one nothing about how teachers and students use them every day. Strangely, little research backs up these beliefs: Do students learn more and better? What purposes does ICT serve in the classroom? These questions about the return on technological investments—have computers done what their champions said they would do?—have gone unasked.

PATTERNS OF TECHNOLOGY USE IN SCHOOLS SINCE THE 1990S

With students and teachers steadily gaining greater access to ICT than to any previous technological innovation, how do they use machines for teaching and learning? What have been the outcomes of use for teachers and students? Our answers to these questions follow.[12]

Limited Use of Computers in Classroom Instruction

Teacher and student use of ICT at home and in school is widespread for doing assignments, preparing lessons, searching the Internet, and using e-mail but lags far behind in routine use for classroom instruction. Except for online instruction in many high schools and reports of programs with 1:1 student–computer ratios (hereafter, simply 1:1 ratio), researchers who observe classrooms have found less than 10% of teachers integrated ICT seamlessly into their lessons on at least a weekly basis. Occasional teacher use of ICT—once a month—had slightly increased in the past decade to nearly 50%, meaning that the percentage of teachers who hardly ever use ICT for classroom instruction remains at around 40%. Even with these modest changes, classroom use of ICT remains, at best, limited.[13]

A recent study of classroom instruction in three districts (Arlington, Virginia; Oakland, California; and Denver, Colorado) between 1993 and 2005 offers systemwide snapshots of technology use. In this study, the researcher collected 1,044 direct observations—not survey responses—of what elementary and secondary schoolteachers in these districts did in their classrooms. These reported observations included summaries of supervisor visits, student descriptions, journalist visits, actual photos, direct classroom observations, and other sources. In effect, these were snapshots of lessons in progress. All instances of technologies being used as part of their lessons were identified, such as use of overhead projectors, videos, LCD projectors, calculators, and, of course, computers in classrooms, media centers, and labs. The summary results show fairly high percentages of teachers using technology (Table 4.1).[14] However, a closer look at specific technology usage reveals that computers were indeed used, but at a very

Table 4.1. Technology use in three school districts, 1993–2005.

	Arlington	*Denver*	*Oakland*
ELEMENTARY	N = 379	N = 68	N = 49
Reports of technology use	N = 75 (20%)	N = 15 (21%)	N = 8 (15%)
SECONDARY	N = 220	N = 166	N = 162
Reports of technology use	N = 105 (48%)	N = 50 (30%)	N = 42 (26%)
TOTAL REPORTS	N = 599	N = 234	N = 211
TOTAL REPORTS OF TECHNOLOGY USE	N = 180 (30%)	N = 65 (28%)	N = 50 (24%)

low rate, and in two districts, less frequently than were overhead projectors (Table 4.2).

In looking solely at ICT used for classroom instruction, percentages of teacher use across the three districts range from 8 to 12%. These results show teachers using mixes of old and new technologies with their students to meet learning objectives. They tell us nothing, however, about frequency of student use, how computers were used in lessons, or their effects on student learning.

To sum up, in over a decade student and teacher access to ICT has expanded dramatically in pursuit of a 1:1 ratio. The digital gap in schools has shrunk considerably in public schools. But gaining access—and this is a crucial

Table 4.2. Technologies used in three school districts, 1993–2005.

	Arlington	*Denver*	*Oakland*
ELEMENTARY REPORTS	N = 379	N = 68	N = 49
Overhead projector	N = 23 (6%)	N = 3 (4%)	N = 3 (6%)
Computers in labs or classrooms	N = 31 (8%)	N = 8 (12%)	N = 3 (6%)
Video/LCD	N = 12 (3%)	N = 3 (4%)	N = 1 (1%)
Calculators	N = 6 (2%)	N = 1 (1%)	N = 1 (2%)
Video camera	N = 1 (less than 1%)		
Audiotapes	N = 2 (less than 1%)		
SECONDARY REPORTS	N = 220	N = 166	N = 162
Overhead projector	N = 49 (22%)	N = 14 (8%)	N = 13 (8%)
Computers in labs or classrooms	N = 2 (10%)	N = 20 (12%)	N = 10 (6%)
Video/LCD	N = 22 (10%)	N = 9 (5%)	N = 13 (8%)
Calculators	N = 6 (3%)	N = 6 (4%)	N = 6 (4%)
Slide projector	N = 1 (less than 1%)		
Audiotapes	N = 5 (2%)	N = 1 (1%)	
TOTALS	N = 599	N = 234	N = 211
Overhead projectors	N = 72 (12%)	N = 17 (7%)	N = 16 (8%)
Computers in labs or classrooms	N = 53 (9%)	N = 28 (12%)	N = 13 (6%)
Video/LCD	N = 34 (6%)	N = 12 (5%)	N = 14 (7%)
Calculators	N = 12 (2%)	N = 7 (3%)	N = 7 (3%)
Other	N = 9 (1%)	N = 1 (less than 1%)	

point—does not necessarily translate into teachers and students routinely using ICT during lessons. And it says nothing about student outcomes. Most schoolteachers have yet to use ICT with their students as often as they use overhead projectors or textbooks.[15]

Few Changes in Pedagogy

Few marked changes in pedagogy have occurred as a result of abundant ICT access. In the early 1980s, Seymour Papert and others predicted the demise of traditional teaching practices as the desktop computer became common in classrooms. Champions of student-centered or constructivist pedagogy latched onto ICT as a means of reducing the dominant and traditional teacher-centered forms of instruction. Yet much data revealed that the introduction of ICT, even with coaching and technical support, had not altered mainstream pedagogies of more than 5% to 10% of teachers. When changes in teaching did occur alongside increased use of ICT—such as with project-based learning —more often than not, they occurred because teacher beliefs and predispositions had already tilted toward student-centered pedagogy.

For example, suppose that a teacher not only believed strongly in children learning a lot in small groups and working on an interdisciplinary project but also felt that loads of writing encouraged student thinking. Suppose further that the teacher designed and implemented these activities well before she had ever used computers in her classroom. Chances are that with a computer at home and some help from technically inclined colleagues, she would use ICT in school labs and her classroom to create teams working on interdisciplinary projects and have students edit drafts multiple times using word-processing software. Most teachers, however, lack those dispositions and supports that tilt toward student-centered instruction.[16]

Furthermore, some researchers have studied how massive infusions of technology do not necessarily translate into teachers altering their daily practices even when 1:1 ratio exists. Consider the work of Judith Sandholtz and her colleagues on the Apple Classroom of Tomorrow (ACOT) program between 1985 and 1998, one of the most extensive studies ever done of computers in classrooms.[17]

The original ACOT project distributed two desktop computers (one for home and one for school) to every student and teacher in five elementary and secondary classrooms across the country, eventually expanding to hundreds of classrooms and schools. ACOT researchers reported student engagement, collaboration, and independent work much as researchers who study 1:1 computer–student ratios do today. But they also found that for teachers to use computers as learning tools, 1:1 ratio was not necessary. In elementary and secondary classrooms, clusters of computers were sufficient to achieve the same level of weekly use and maintain the other tasks that teachers and students had to accomplish.[18]

With some teachers but not the majority, teacher-centered practices shifted slowly to student-centered ones, over years—as long as teachers worked closely together and had sufficient technical on-site support. On-site professional development, whereby teachers learned from one another, made a significant difference in shifting practices, again, over many years. What ACOT researchers found was that, over time, as teachers worked through the different stages of technology use, they created hybrids of student- and teacher-centered practices, using computers for certain activities and not others.[19]

ACOT demonstrated clearly that dumping a lot of equipment into classrooms would not magically change teaching; many other things need to come together for teachers to alter their pedagogy to promote learning. So there is little question that teachers—male and female, old and young—use ICT as personal learning tools at home and at school in lesson research and preparation, e-mail, and administrative tasks. Nor is there any question that teachers see computers as helpful to their students' motivation and daily work in schools. Yet as long as teachers are expected to pursue the many purposes of public schooling such as civic, moral, and job preparation—through maintaining control of students in classrooms; making certain that students are respectful, fair, and complete their work; and ensuring that students achieve district and state standards as measured by tests—abundant access to new technologies can create mixes of teaching practices but will hardly transform pedagogy, even in a 1:1 ratio model.

No Causal Link Between ICT Access and Student Gains

Abundant ICT access and small gains in teacher use have yet to reveal any causal link to students' improved academic achievement. Beginning in the early 1960s, a number of projects began using computer-assisted instruction (CAI) whereby students would sit at terminals and scroll through a series of reading and math lessons, insert answers to questions, and take periodic tests embedded in the lessons to determine if they understood the content and could perform the skills. Students would then take standardized achievement tests in reading and math. Researchers designed studies that compared students doing math and reading in traditional classrooms with those doing CAI.

Analyses and meta-analyses of these studies over the years showed that CAI did yield gains in test scores. However, after intensive examination of these meta-analyses, researchers found that in studies where the same teacher taught the control group and the experimental group, the difference between the scores of students in the computer-using group and the scores of students in the non-computer-using group were not as great as when two different teachers taught the control and experimental groups. Without controls on teachers' instructional approaches, test scores varied greatly. Thus, while teachers affect student learning, their effects are lost in the muddled design of most studies of computer use. Research design is discussed further below.[20]

Except for the initial glowing results for CAI (and eventual downsizing of these claims) and some evidence for improved writing as a result of using ICT, for the past 80 years of research on technology's impact on learning, not much reliable evidence has emerged to give impartial observers confidence that K–12 students' use of computers or any other electronic device leads directly to improved literacy as measured by reading and math test scores. Of course, putting this so bluntly contradicts vendor ads, software developer claims, and federal officials' pronouncements. Attributing test score gains to increased use of ICT has been around for nearly a century and is, at best, misleading and, at worst, false.[21] And the snake oil can be costly in more ways than one.

Some recent examples of misattribution might help. For example, a small district in Alaska and another in New Jersey enrolling largely poor minority students have continually been championed as sterling models of places where extensive purchase and use of computers have led to substantial gains in test scores. What is often omitted from these accounts, however, is that each district received extensive increases in funding and launched systemwide reforms in curriculum, teaching, and accountability 3–5 years before schools were wired and computers bought. Yet gains in academic achievement were attributed to computers, not the funding or deep structural and curricular reforms introduced years earlier.[22]

What causes enthusiasts to attribute gains in achievement to ICT use (and one can easily see this syndrome of attribution in earlier studies of classroom use of film and instructional television, including ACOT and recent studies of 1:1 ratios in particular districts) is the design error whereby researchers confuse the medium of instruction (instructional television or laptops) with the instructional method embedded in the software and the teacher's approaches to the lesson?

Richard Clark and others have said for decades that instructional television, personal computers, laptops, and handheld devices are vehicles for transporting instructional methods. But they are not neutral tools, and they are not the pedagogy itself. What we mean by pedagogy is instructional methods such as teacher questioning, giving examples, lecture, recitation, guided discussion, drill, cooperative learning, individualized instruction, simulations, tutoring, project-based learning, and innumerable variations and combinations of these teaching practices and approaches.

Confounding ICT with teaching methods in designing research studies has produced misleading results and missed the importance of which methods are more efficient in learning, that is, produce similar results at less cost.

Or as Clark candidly put it: Media like television, film, and computers "deliver instruction but do not influence student achievement any more than the truck that delivers our groceries causes changes in our nutrition."[23]

To press home the basic point that ICT has been entangled with instructional methods influencing learning, Clark uses a medical analogy—of an antibiotic prescribed by a doctor to get rid of a serious infection. The antibiotic comes in tablets, liquids, or injection. Each of these can deliver the active ingredient in the antibiotic that will reduce the fever, kill bacteria, and end the infection. The active ingredient in the antibiotic is comparable to the method of instruction, not whether it is swallowed as a pill, sipped as a liquid, or injected. Although the efficiency of how the antibiotic is taken is important to know, it would be irrelevant to argue whether tablets or liquids will lower the fever and kill bacteria, yet that is what happens when researchers confuse how something is delivered with the active ingredient. Switch now to computers and test scores.

Misleading results, however, do not come only from a research design that confuses the medium with teacher pedagogy. Misleading results also come from two interrelated issues: confusing correlations with causation by both researchers and policymakers, and attributing learning to computer use. In terms of causation versus correlation, consider test scores. Time and again, when studies report student use of computers and gains in test scores, journalists, vendors, and policymakers attribute those gains to computer use. Take the massive Program for International Student Assessment (PISA) surveys of nearly 100,000 15-year-olds from 32 countries in 2000. That study reported that students with access to a computer at home and at school also did well on tests. The correlation was pumped up to a cause–effect relationship by national policymakers and promoters of ICT in those nations that had already invested public funds in wiring schools and purchasing hardware. Then, a few years later, along came other researchers who took the same PISA results and, controlling for certain family and educational variables in their regression analysis, concluded that in some cases access to computers lowered test scores and in other cases had no significant influence on scores. In both the original PISA study and its subsequent reanalysis, the results are correlations and cannot be construed as computers causing scores to rise or fall.[24]

Attributing learning to the use of computers arises time and again in the design of research studies. The typical study of laptops, for example, compares test scores of students who have classroom laptops with those of students who lack them. In those few studies that try to control for socioeconomic and academic differences among students, test scores, attitudes toward schools, motivation, attendance, and other outcomes turn out more positive for students who have laptops.[25]

In terms of use versus learning, few, if any, studies ever hold constant the teacher—that is, the same teacher for laptop and nonlaptop classes—or ever isolate and examine how teachers teach during the time of the study. The focus is on the machines. And this is why it is impossible to conclude that test scores rose *because students used ICT*. It is what Clark and others have said for decades: Confusing the truck delivering the food and eating a nutritious diet; confusing the taking of a pill or a liquid for the active ingredient. Researcher-designed studies confound ICT—the medium—with the teacher's instructional methods and report time and again initial gains in test scores that are then attributed to laptops, not what and how the teacher teaches.

To sum up for outcomes of abundant access to and use of ICT, no widespread changes in teaching or test score gains have occurred. For those studies that do claim such shifts in classroom pedagogies or gains in scores due to ICT, we have argued that a fundamental confusion between medium and method of instruction leads to making misattributions about the effects of technology on academic achievement.

In answering the three questions, we asked about patterns of teaching amid abundant access to ICT. But we have said little about the recent surge of 1:1 ratios in schools around the nation. So another question arises: With the spread of 1:1 ratios in public schools—and the absolute ubiquity of ICT—will the patterns we have noted in teacher and student use continue, and will those outcomes affecting pedagogy and achievement, as measured by test scores, persist?

1:1 RATIOS IN PUBLIC SCHOOLS

Let's look more closely at computer use in schools. Has frequency of student use increased in classrooms? According to teacher, student, and administrator surveys and interviews about laptop programs, the answer is an unqualified yes. Survey results are slowly accumulating that teachers and students report using computers more often than when they had access to fewer computers in the classrooms, mobile carts, labs, and media centers.

But how much more use and what kinds of use? No clear answers have yet to surface. Newspaper accounts and many teacher, student, and parent surveys of programs with 1:1 ratios in Maine, Henrico County (Virginia), and individual districts scattered across the nation report extraordinary enthusiasm. Teachers report daily use of laptops and elevated student interest in schoolwork, higher motivation from previously lackluster students, and more engagement in lessons. Students and parents report similar high levels of use and interest in learning. All of these enthusiastic responses to programs with 1:1 ratios have a déjà vu feel to those of us who have heard similar gusto for technological innovations prior to the novelty wearing off.[26]

The déjà vu feeling is not only from knowing the history of classroom machines; it is also because the evidence is largely drawn from self-reports. Surely, some of these self-reports of enthusiastic teachers mirror accounts by journalists and others who describe outstanding teachers who have incorporated laptops and other technologies into an elaborate repertoire of teaching approaches. Other reporters have observed teachers in their classrooms who raised serious questions about reliance on laptops to carry most of the curriculum and instructional load. Those reports by people who actually sit in classrooms and observe daily teaching, unfortunately, are uncommon. Mostly, results on classroom use come from questionnaires that teachers complete and interviews. And researchers know the dangers of unreliable estimates that plague survey and interview responses. Investigators who have examined the classrooms of teachers and students who reported high usage have found large discrepancies between what was reported and what was observed. So a healthy dose of skepticism about teacher claims of daily use and students' long-term engagement are in order because few researchers have directly observed classroom lessons in which students use laptops for sustained periods of time. Until more direct observation studies emerge from classrooms, it will be hard to say with confidence that teachers' daily use of computers has changed considerably with programs with 1:1 ratios.[27]

Nor can we say with confidence that a transformation in classroom practice has occurred as a result of 1:1 ratios. Surely, promoters of 1:1 ratios have made the claim. Rather than give extended quotes, we offer a typical one from a review of programs with 1:1 ratios in various districts: "Collaborative learning, rigorous authentic learning, inquiry-based learning, and active, engaged learning are consistently associated with 1 to 1 learning initiatives." Repeating *learning* five times in the same sentence is a bit much, but the reviewers concluded, without reservation, that 1:1 ratios would transform pedagogy. The earlier discussion of ACOT suggested that such changes could occur but would take an extended period of time; would require much on-site professional development, technical support, and teacher collaboration; and would occur more frequently among teachers who are already predisposed to nontraditional ways of teaching.[28]

And what about outcomes of 1:1 ratios among teachers and students? As the above discussion on the persistent pattern of research designs confounding machines with teaching methods suggested, correlations of gains in literacy and achievement test scores with 1:1 ratios will continue to be reported in journals and the popular media. Vendors and promoters of laptops will ensure that outcome. But such results are spurious, since they do not (and cannot) show a causal link between laptop use and a rise in test scores.

Too often, discussions of access, use, and outcomes ignore the institutional mission and other factors that often shape what and how teachers teach and students learn. Even though the promotion of computers stems from a business-inspired view of schools helping to keep the economy strong, not to mention the factor of ensuring intergenerational markets, teachers' decisions about what content and skills to teach and how to teach ultimately determine what old and new technologies get used in their rooms and to what degree literacy is enhanced by ICT.

What should be clear to readers thus far is that how libraries and schools have adopted and used new technologies differed considerably in the past half-century. Chapter 5 shows these differences in two literacy-advancing tax-supported community institutions.

CHAPTER 5

Schools and Libraries as Partners in Community Technologies: Special Projects or Permanent Promise?

Even with so many institutional and political constraints, and after nearly two centuries, public schools and libraries continue to operate as separated partners in promoting and "guarding" literacy, especially in offering new technologies to patrons and students. They have developed as neighboring guardians, cultivating their own populations, but largely independent of each other. Library educator Kathleen de la Pena McCook focuses on the disadvantages of their disconnection from each other and from the larger public discussion on community:

> The geographical nature of much of the landscape of places where people live in the United States has provoked discussion and proposals to build community. Librarians have been part of the discussion but not part of the proposals. . . . The status of libraries in the ongoing national dialogue on community is somewhat analogous to that of public schools—often perceived as a closed system because of inherent organization structures. Yet, libraries have been spectacularly successful in reconfiguring services in a period of rapid technological growth, and at the same time maintaining credibility in providing for community space.[1]

We need to discuss how schools and libraries can perform their historic role in communities in better ways. How can both of these community-based institutions nurture literacy in communities? Pilot projects of schools and libraries in communities may carry more of the answers than national think tanks and pundits have offered.

According to a 2006 study commissioned by the Gates Foundation, a majority of the public felt that libraries and schools were doing "good" to "excellent" jobs and that the quality of public education was a high priority for their communities. But the public also felt that some major areas of improvement were that youth and adult literacy populations needed good programs and places to study. While many suggestions were given for improvement, practically nothing was said about partnering with schools apart from increasing Internet access in them.[2]

Yet in Los Angeles, Seattle, Chicago, New York, and other cities, public libraries have forged ahead to partner with schools and other agencies to advance literacy and renew communities. In the Pico-Union neighborhood in Los Angeles, for example, the branch library sponsors "coffee and conversation" for the over-65 residents. The event brings together strangers and neighbors to talk about city politics, the Middle East conflict, immigration, and other newsworthy topics. In Chinatown, newcomers enter the recently built branch for a weekly citizenship class at which they prepare for the test by yelling out to the teacher answers to questions about the Constitution, the three branches of government, and the Bill of Rights. At the new Ascot branch library in the middle of the gritty neighborhood near Florence and Main Streets, 13-year-old Joseph Robinson and 9-year-old Franklin Flores are in their favorite corner in front of a computer terminal playing RuneScape together. During the summer, they are mainstays there, enraptured by the software game.[3]

These examples illustrate that libraries can become bridge institutions that build networks of strangers to create what Robert Putnam and others have called "social capital"—people willing to help and trust one another—to revitalize a neighborhood, renew a school, and broker community rebuilding. But libraries and schools, together, do more than build social capital. In fostering literacy in the community, they become engaged in a democratic process of building a community-minded culture.[4]

We believe that a locally grown and informed perspective is needed for community-based education and literacy through technologies, aside from top-down projects to stock libraries and schools with more Internet-connected computers. After all, "electronic and digital resources are very attractive, even seductive, but merely possessing them is not a mission."[5] Let's look at a potential framework.[6]

A SOCIAL PRACTICE LENS FOR COMMUNITY-BASED EDUCATION AND LITERACY

Suppose we view people becoming literate in many different places—in their homes, neighborhoods, schools, libraries, neighborhood organizations, places of worship, and workplaces. Seen this way, literacy practices grow out of groups interacting daily in the family, in schools, on the street, in the mosque, and in the workplace as individuals learn from one another. Children learn from parents, uncles, grandparents, cousins, and neighbors. Job newcomers are inducted by old-timers and, in doing so, individuals as well as groups shift roles and relationships as they observe one another and solve problems together. In academic jargon, this learning from one another in groups is called "communities of practice." But they don't interact in a vacuum; the community, institution, and larger society—with all of the technological panoply available—impinge upon home, school, neighborhood, church, and workplace.[7]

Some examples of literacy practices within institutions may help. If a teacher at a school believes that her e-mails are being monitored, she may write certain things or not write much at all on the school computer. A library patron, knowing that filters have recently been installed, may act similarly. Literacy practices are also reflective of new social practices; for example, new words may exist in e-mails and on blog sites that are not in other types of documents. Or literacy practices may be mundane, as with ritualistic activities that people perform automatically, such as a student who "accepts" a receipt of his teacher's memo on his e-mail system just as if he had received a regular letter. Literacy, then, is in-action and moves with people in their communities and environments.[8]

The important point is that literacy, like people's social practices, is differentially situated because of the community and the institutions in which they occur. Each institution brands its literacy practices. Schools have been associated with an autonomous view of literacy focusing on reading and writing as a technical skill and with a strong emphasis on academic outcomes and preparation for the workplace. Schools, moreover, instruct in groups as students move through an age-graded system. This autonomous approach has been carried over into the deployment of personal computers in elementary and secondary schools to boost children's academic achievement. Yet, as we have seen, the mission of school stretches well beyond academic achievement, and, subsequently, these computers may be less used for classroom instruction.[9]

Public libraries, alternatively, carry a range of literacies and languages (English and non-English), including technologically based literacy. In this sense, they offer "multiple literacies" to individual patrons.[10] Multiple literacies offer more than an autonomous approach to reading in one context or as a purely mechanical activity.[11] Some multiple literacies are:

- *Critical literacy*. Reading and writing as a politically charged activity that challenges social conventions and institutions, and proposes social and political changes, such as at the Highlander Center.[12]

- *Digital literacy.* Reading and writing through electronic formats; being able to critically analyze and integrate electronic information, including using data to experiment, creating databases, creating web pages, and desktop publishing.
- *Environmental literacy.* Engagement with "green" issues and sustainability of the environment, such as global warming, as well as questioning mainstream scientific knowledge.[13]
- *Health literacy.* Being able to read and write a range of health messages; manage personal health and critically analyze health care; and address health barriers, as well as cultural, age, gender, and race issues with regard to health.[14]

This list of literacies also includes academic literacy (critical use and experiences of writing for academic purposes), information literacy (locating, using, and critically evaluating diverse information sources), visual literacy (being able to design, identify, and critically evaluate images), media literacy (critical analysis of mass media messages), and multicultural literacy (cultural competence with diverse written narratives). It can also include lifelong learning skills such as financial literacy (ability to critically evaluate and use economics in daily life). Clearly, literacy practices, like social practices, evolve, especially as they engage technology.[15]

Public libraries, due to their constant use of print and nonprint sources and new technologies, educate their diverse patrons in a number of these literacies on an ongoing basis—from printed books, to audio books, to the Internet. Libraries offer more and different kinds of literacy, even supporting types that have gone underground in other institutions like schools.[16] Highlighting these are important, since schools and school libraries focus almost entirely on academic and information literacies, with in-school librarians helping students find resources for their assignments, teaching them forms of citation, and making them aware of Internet sources. Students say they get better grades as a result and do schoolwork better.[17] Yet school librarians have diminished in numbers because of cutbacks and have often been replaced by aides and nonprofessionals. Public libraries are better funded; they are also more accessible and flexible than school libraries in terms of hours and days of operation. They also attract many different types of publics, including families. Schools and libraries can complement each other with community-based technologies, based on their literacy missions.

COMPLEMENTARY ROLES FOR LIBRARIES AND SCHOOLS

While libraries and schools share common missions, they have different roles, allowing them to cultivate many literacies in communities. When they are expected to work together in a partnership, leaders talk about their roles in very pragmatic terms ("how-to's" that lead to discrete outcomes), not in terms of forming a community of practice of learners. For example, the American Library Association (ALA) recommends making a sequential list of activities so that libraries can build "a community of readers through partnerships and technology." These steps and tasks consist of knowing "useful facts" about schools; mapping community assets; and knowing the missions, needs, and goals of other organizations. The recommendations that flow from this advice call for librarians to prepare handouts for five to ten community organizations, "write the directors, do your homework, repeat the process." These cookie-cutter methods characterize these partnering projects, with their main rationale being to reduce costs through sharing resources as part of better management, leadership, and organization.[18] Although these partnership models may well be organized and expedient, they ignore local issues such as transforming education into a communitywide literacy program. In addition, too often skimpy institutional analysis occurs, apart from whether or not the partnership is deemed successful. It is as if the institution and people's roles within it are mere backdrops for the project, rather than dynamic centers mediating its effects.[19]

KEY FACTORS FOR CONSIDERING PARTNERSHIPS BETWEEN SCHOOLS AND LIBRARIES

To examine deeper and sustained institutional partnerships aimed at promoting community literacy using new technologies, we analyze *populations* (rural, new immigrants, low-income, women and girls, at-risk teens); *purposes* (voluntary versus mandatory education), *processes* (types of learning and literacies), and *knowledge* (technical and narrative).

Populations

There has been a decided shift in library populations from mostly children and their mothers, who used to dominate patron statistics, to people of all ages (including seniors) and immigrants.[20]

Rural, semirural, and transitional communities. In rural, semirural, and transitional areas, technology access in libraries and schools tends to be lower due to fewer resources, although recent private gifts (e.g., "packages" of Microsoft software) have helped somewhat. Even with limited access, one study found that rural library patrons in general tend to go online more often than urban and suburban patrons.[21] Yet these same communities are considered at risk for losing these new resources due to onetime donations drying up with no replacement funds and lack of technical expertise when computers crash. These conditions are further exacerbated because these libraries are isolated and have modest budgets and few staff.[22] Many Native American reservations, for example, have schools filled with new technologies, but outside of the schools they lack basic infrastructure for technology, including connectivity. A study found that in New Mexico home computer ownership is approximately 10%, making libraries and schools the only places to offer access to computers because of their discounted telecommunications subsidies. Rural adult populations often need basic information for which technology can help them, such as health advice and access to medical assistance. But rural patrons also use computers for printing out reports, résumés, and job ads, and for finding out local news—all of which makes educational programming important. A rural-sustainability project funded by the Gates Foundation trains library staff to develop action plans for building capacity in their computing services and programs. Technology support, upgrade and maintenance of technology, staff and patron training, outreach, and advocacy were identified as supports that are needed but lacking.[23] There has been little attention, however, to how technology can help rural libraries and schools allocate their limited resources to genuinely benefit isolated populations.[24]

Teens. Youth between the ages of 12 and 17 were found to use the Internet much more than adults (87% compared to 66%). Yet youth who lack access are more likely to come from low-income families (those earning under $30,000)—only 73% compared to 90% of those from families with higher incomes. While many teens go online at home, over half do so at the library, up from 36 percent in 2000. Hispanic and African American teens have been found to depend on the library more for computer access than White youth.[25]

Youth use library computers to conduct research, do homework, play games, and participate in volunteer projects to help adults. Young people view library computers as not only information-seeking hubs but also as socializing centers that include learning opportunities.[26] One survey found that while librarians were committed to serving teens, most offer reading and cultural programs aimed heavily at elementary-age children, not high school students. They also seldom provide computer skills training, homework help centers, or career exploration. Libraries can offer more "multimodal literacies" to teens[27] than test-oriented high schools. Alternative literacy activities for teens can potentially include (but are not limited to) reading and creating e-zines, videogaming, blogging, and website design. These are supportive of academic literacies in that they are powerful learning tools. They are also supportive of non-school-based literacies.

The Brooklyn Public Library, for example, trains librarians to deal with the developmental needs of children and teens. They have consulted with a teen advisory group and a focus group to create math tutoring programs and a reading program called Book Buddies as well as computer classes.[28] An academic school–library partnership in Seattle allows volunteers and paid specialists from the community to give online homework help to students. They also make referrals, provide information on further web links, read teacher comments, edit essays, and provide feedback about student presentations. Students can log on every day and receive assistance, even in Spanish. Those with learning disabilities also receive help through school–library partnerships. This is a case where outside professionals can make a difference with technology. They serve as liaisons, teachers, and consultants and can fill in gaps of expertise and resources.[29]

Libraries, however, do more than provide homework assistance. They focus on youth development. As some authors note, "teens do not grow up in programs but in families and communities." In a sense, libraries are "nonjudgmental" places for teens to feel like they belong and "hang out," as one teen expressed in a study.[30]

New immigrant communities. The arrival of immigrants has diversified many rural and semirural communities. Yet many of these communities' services may not be set up to best serve immigrants' needs. Bilingual education, for example, is now defunct in a number of states. Libraries can at least partially compensate by offering technological resources and programs in native languages and bilingual programming.

Yet technology is usually not considered in library services to immigrant communities, but it may be important in light of major income and language gaps. Many libraries, for example, offer English for Speakers of Other Languages (ESOL) software in their literacy programs as well as dual-language family literacy kits for parents, families, schools, and community organizations.[31]

Computer access with multimedia capabilities may be particularly important for staying in touch with family and news in their home country. The Cyber Centers in Arlington (Virginia), for example, tailor their computer services to large new immigrant populations in this way. Libraries that intentionally increase their computer capacity seem to attract immigrant populations, as one librarian in Greensboro (North Carolina) who participated in a study to increase adult literacy through technology found. Libraries are often seen as computer centers by this population, and the task is to engage new immigrant communities in other aspects of the library. In addition, acquiring Americorps, Volunteers in Service to America (VISTA), and other trained staff can help facilitate the use of computers and provide bridges to schools and other organizations.[32]

Women immigrants in particular have had less access to technology. Many women are in households with low incomes, and only 20% were found to use the Internet for any activity on a regular basis in one Montreal (Canada) study. One Canadian study found that many women immigrants access computers from a public location and use them for communicating with friends and family. They were also more likely to use them for career purposes than the general population.[33]

Girls and women. Although libraries were originally designed for working-class men, women and their children have consistently constituted the main population of library users for nearly a century. Libraries have always been predominantly female environments. Since libraries operate according to demand (with regard to circulation of books and people), women patrons historically used this to their advantage in regard to reading fiction. Yet, with the introduction of computers into libraries, there has been a gender shift, with technologies attracting men and boys.[34] Less attention, in fact, has been paid to gender in the digital gap debates, although studies have located clear disparities between males and females in terms of physical access, amount of time, skills and knowledge, formal education or training, and types of computer use. Some of this disparity, of course, is in terms of actual usage. Studies show that males and females use the Internet about equally in the United States,[35] and female attitudes and achievement scores in reading and math are similar to those of males. In addition, public and school librarians, still heavily female fields, are technologically proficient with ICT, and teachers—also, a female-dominated profession—have been found to use computers as much as males.

Yet inequalities still exist, especially with regard to education and training, and in a world that is increasingly competitive, without proper sponsorship, women could be even more disadvantaged. Libraries working together with schools may be able to turn around these disparities, although there have not been any major known projects specifically for this purpose.[36]

Purposes

While lifelong learning is both a library slogan and a school aspiration, a key difference between schools and libraries is that the former is compulsory while use of the latter is voluntary. One of the major reasons for this is that schools' main clients are children who have to attend, while libraries serve both children and adults who choose to come. Due to serving many different publics, the library has become more of a multipurpose agency, providing different activities and materials for different populations. This compulsory–voluntary difference shapes institutional norms with regard to technology uses and the content of learning.

With community-based education, however, these purposes blur, as when schools expect parents to get more involved in schools, in after-school programs, and in homework projects; a New York City initiative called Learning in Libraries, for example, is an after-school collaborative effort focused on reading, acquiring more resources, and advancing academic literacies.[37]

Through federal grants—including the Technology Literacy Challenge Fund (bringing new computers into schools, connecting them to the Internet, developing software, and training teachers), Technology Innovation Challenge Grant (focusing on building community partnerships through technology in neighborhoods and across institutions), and Community Technology Centers (establishing computer learning centers in low-income organizations)—the focus is on disseminating technology into schools, libraries, and other community institutions. These federally funded projects equate technology with education, which can, in turn, mesh the purposes of schools and libraries in fundamentally new ways. While it is important that these projects receive initial federal financial support, for these programs to be sustained over time, libraries, schools, families, and community leaders and organizations have to be informed and involved both in implementation and in lobbying local officials for continued funding.

Indeed, technology blurs boundaries in school and library purposes on a community level. For example, the Schools of Thought project focuses on restructuring curriculum and instruction, even bringing in community organizations, in ways that focus on "competencies and confidence necessary for success in the 21st century."[38] This project focuses on establishing a community of learners among teachers and children as they work through various goals of the group. Students conduct research and share it with other publics, as is done at universities. They also focus on collaborative problem solving with video and for adventures. There is much opportunity for feedback and reflection, especially through peers and critical dialogue. Assessments focus on the path of the students as they follow the project through the year to see about their performance. Most importantly, the project focuses on building communities in and outside of the classroom—including parents, administrators, college students, and business representatives. Through computer-mediated communication (from videoconferencing, to computer-based simulations, to the interactive aspects of the Internet), the students are able to learn through active participation. In this case, technology shifts the purposes of schools to becoming more inclusive.

Yet if schools lack this capacity, libraries in many communities may be able to fill such a role as a supplement for schools, as in after-school programs or programs for out-of-school youth. Teachers, students, and parents alike (for better or worse) see the General Educational Development (GED) test, for example, as a viable option for achieving a high school credential. More and more GED courses in adult basic education attract higher levels of young adults. Thus more literacy programs, including those in libraries, may start to acquire online forms of the GED to complement their print-based

GED materials to make it more accessible and self-directed. These actions, however, have not yet happened on a large scale.[39]

In fact, libraries for some youth may be the only place they receive any type of education, especially in rural areas. Near Houston (Texas), one library system trains low-income youth to become leaders in guiding library services, including technology, and they call them "Tech Teens." They get paid for tutoring younger children in churches and other youth organizations, where space is provided for computers and other technology as part of their activities. At the Philadelphia Free Library, which has a Learn, Enjoy, and Play (LEAP) after-school program, teens advise librarians and create websites. The teens' learning interests are met in unique ways.[40]

Other libraries focus on at-risk students in school and incorporate study skills in their program. In Baltimore, the Enoch Pratt Free Library integrates technology into various aspects of its youth programming to include homework assistance, customer service, and mentoring younger students. These high school students receive community service credits toward graduation. Due to their multipurpose function, libraries can enhance social networks of the community, instill information and technological literacy, and encourage independent learning.[41]

Still, public schools remain the largest providers of after-school programs. These programs have grown to meet the demands of many families who choose them because of their low cost, convenience, and children's enjoyment. According to one survey, 53% of African American and 40% of Hispanic parents would enroll their children if such a program were available, with 23% of Caucasian families endorsing this option. These parents believe that their children would have fun, stay out of trouble, receive academic enrichment, and improve their social skills as well as their physical health and fitness.[42] Technology is used in many of these after-school programs and is a main purpose of the 21st-century community learning centers.[43] One study found that 95% of parents felt their children would benefit from after-school programs if they had computers.

Processes

Differential learning activities. Learning activities, whether on computers or not, differ in libraries and schools. Differences occur because of divergent instructional approaches and state and federal academic mandates. Institutional roles also account for differences. Libraries and library literacy programs rely heavily on one-to-one learning and self-directed learning, while public schools organize teaching mostly in groups, with independent learning as a subordinate activity except in computer labs, where learning is often individualized. Since the early 1990s, state and district testing and accountability regulations—particularly after 2002, when the federal No Child Left Behind Act became law—have intensified schools' attention upon all students becoming literate across reading, math, science, and other subjects on a grade-by-grade schedule.

Not to be ignored are the pronounced social-class disparities in public schools that shape children's learning opportunities. One study by Henry Becker in 2000 found that schools with high percentages of children of low socioeconomic status (SES) had more drill-and-skill software programs than did schools where most of the children were middle or upper middle class, and that in English and mathematics, students in predominantly low-SES schools used such programs more often than did students in predominantly higher SES schools. In Hawai'i, Mark Warchauer found that in two schools, both with extensive technology access and reputations for good practices, the high-SES school prepared students to be scholars and focused on project-based learning, used advanced equipment, and emphasized critical thinking and problem solving in real settings to understand complex phenomena, whereas the low-SES school emphasized simple activities and focused on students' feelings, emphasized behavioral discipline, and prepared students for employment. While both projects were deemed as "educational" by the researcher and teachers, the kinds of classroom practices using technology reflected the institution's socially derived views of what is appropriate for different students.[44]

Other studies have found that high-SES schools tend to emphasize whole language in reading, constructivist-based learning, creativity, experiential learning, computer-mediated instruction, and critical thinking skills that prepare students for academic goals, along with providing well-resourced libraries, while low-SES schools focus on phonics, direct instruction, simple tasks, and low-level types of skills.[45]

Some school-based projects attempt to change these unequal practices. Higher-order thinking skills (HOTS), for example, concentrate on using computers to teach low-income children metacognitive skills. Laboratories are set up specifically for this purpose, and computer-mediated learning replaces the computer-assisted or computer-based learning that would normally predominate.[46] School libraries are involved, but how could public libraries further enhance these goals?

Public libraries in low-SES communities might be particularly valuable for enriching academic knowledge, metacognitive skills, and emotional development of children through partnering with schools. Many public libraries offer intergenerational programming, including computer-assisted learning that helps to introduce low-income parents and children to technological learning and the pleasure of reading books.[47] The Redwood City Public Library's Project READ, for example, is a program that attempts to unite intergenerational literacy development with computers to foster community literacy through a variety of venues. At the library adult tutors and children with headsets work together on computers to develop their skills and knowledge, and at a local school a small group of parents learn English-language skills using laptops. Computer-assisted learning is also available on-site for parents to develop ESOL skills while their children are in school.

Digital literacies in libraries. Gaming experts claim that many video games, contrary to popular opinion, enhance rather than replace literacy. Video games allow for the sophisticated manipulation of texts, symbols, and images. Gamers can research, debate facts, theorize, build models and maps, and engage in much writing while building intricate and resourceful social networks—all while having fun. Some libraries, for example, have gaming nights for students and have books based on games that are regularly checked out. Libraries can also help low-income families acquire digital literacies. They can also boost skills and training for girls and women. Elisabeth Hayes found that women tend to play more casual video games than serious commercial ones designed in more complex ways. But this was due to a lack of exposure and training, not women's "natural" preference to engage in nonserious videogaming. Therefore, stereotypes about women's lack of interest in video games, or even their abilities to use them, are undeserved. Librarians can receive training themselves and provide a supportive environment for their female patrons to learn.[48]

As schools become more academically oriented and concentrate on measurable objectives that are testable, they are less likely to embrace games than ever before. Libraries, however, have forged ahead with digital literacies through their many learning options. In this sense, library staff position themselves as "literacy-ready" institutions expanding multiple literacies for the community.[49]

Knowledge

Clearly, libraries are known for being cultural, interdisciplinary institutions upholding lifelong learning while guarding the cultural heritages of communities. Yet they are also known as repositories of personal meaning and understanding of the world through their accumulated stories or, as academics put it, narrative knowledge.[50]

Education, then, focuses on the development of narrative competencies in both individuals and communities telling their stories. As Carol Witherell and Nel Noddings put it,

> Stories provide meaning and belonging in our lives. They attach us to others and to our own histories by providing a tapestry rich with threads of time. . . . The story fabric offers us images, myths, metaphors that are morally resonant and contribute to our knowing and being known.[51]

Libraries and schools can help individual communities locate their historical memories, local knowledge, and creativeness. This type of knowledge is different from the logico-scientific knowledge that focuses on abstract rules and principles and prizes categorizing, labeling, and compartmentalizing knowledge.[52] Western education, according to Jerome Bruner, has traditionally followed this trajectory; with the No Child Left Behind Act, more schools are invested in instrumentalist forms of knowledge that elevate the standard knowledge in commercial textbooks and formulaic reading programs emphasizing phonics. This is very different from narrative knowledge, which can free the imagination and loosen creativity. Surely, many kinds of knowledge—narrative, logico-scientific, arts, and humanities—are crucial in forming literate citizens engaged in their communities. Both schools and libraries, as partners in and proponents of diverse literacies for lifelong learning, can move beyond their specialized roles to collaborate better than they have in the past.[53]

Both institutions also demonstrate the potential for partnering to improve community members' persistence in learning, exposure to literacies, and diverse educational opportunities at the local level. It is unclear whether projects can indeed be integrated and transform both the purposes and core functions of the respective institutions. How can schools and libraries join together to produce, embed, and sustain a wider net of literacy practices and knowledge for the community?

TRANSFORMATIVE COLLABORATIONS

Many library–school technology projects are designed to be exploratory or short term. Most of these remain at the project level and do not attempt to reform their institutional structures or foster sustained community-based education. Their main purpose is usually short-term expediency: to share resources due to budget retrenchment or to meet state and federal demands for integration.

Alternatively, transformative collaborations have a shared vision, mission, and goals translated into altered governance and decision making by developing planning strategies and interdisciplinary approaches that support interdependence. They also share resources, and while they may work on concrete endeavors, they are not based purely on pragmatic concerns (e.g., raising money for more literacy programs). Such collaborations would involve a process of institutionalization that sustains community-based education.[54]

While there are numerous manuals that spell out the technical steps of forming collaborations, few discuss how institutional collaborations can be converted into communities of learning with diverse literacy practices. Such collaborations can address urgent needs in society and serve as levers for change, bringing together different publics to enact a joint mission. While they would be designed to meet local everyday needs, they would also require a big-picture outlook that extends across cities and states for restructuring policies and regulations. This process would entail everything from acquiring much financial support to researching, strategizing, planning, and carefully working out stages of implementing innovations. Such partnerships would involve many different community-based education organizations and stakeholders.[55]

One of the fundamental components of transformative collaborations is community-based research (CBR).[56] CBR is conducted with, not for or on, members of a community. Questions driving CBR come from the needs of community members, and the work itself is collaborative and change-oriented. Thus, CBR blends learning and skills development with social action to provide those in a community greater resources and a strong sense of self-efficacy that can lead to future action without the need for outside "experts." It focuses on power sharing, civic efficacy, and participatory decision making among community-based education stakeholders.[57]

Although originating in higher education, CBR has value for libraries and schools engaging in community-based education using technology. Although CBR focuses on four different organizational collaboration models—the solo model, a small CBR program with regular partners, a large and complex community-based center, and a local or regional consortium—it is the last one that packs the most punch because it works on macro- and microlevels. The regional consortium combines and disperses diverse resources and supports, as well as many different kinds of projects with technology that are tailored to neighborhoods.

One example is the Seattle Community Technology Alliance (SCTA), a collaborative effort on part of a number of agencies to develop meaningful and sustainable community technology centers in Seattle. Thirty-five centers link various low-income communities to technology resources that increase their opportunities for learning. It is a collaborative effort of the Seattle Public Library (SPL), Seattle's Department of Information Technology, the Seattle Public Schools, the Chinese Information and Service Center, the Women's Community Impact Consortium, Powerful Schools, the Seattle Housing Authority, the Seattle Department of Parks and Recreation, and various corporations in the area.

The centers, located in established community centers, housing projects, schools, and social service agencies, offer a variety of programs, including after-school activities, adult and family literacy, career development and job preparation, and small business opportunities. To improve the impact, effectiveness, and sustainability of these centers, staff train teenagers to build and maintain the computer labs throughout the summer. This reflects a larger state and city initiative to provide more public-access terminals in many different community-based agencies, including a long-running program between schools and libraries called "Connecting Learners to Libraries."[58]

Three thousand miles away, the Connecting Libraries and Schools Program (CLASP), a technology initiative of schools and libraries in New York, is another example of a long-running collaborative with significant technology programming. Originally funded for three community school districts, CLASP later expanded, through the support of the New York Council, to 13 community school districts citywide, serving students in kindergarten through eighth grade, and three area systems—the Brooklyn Public Library, the New York Public Library, and the Queens Borough Public Library.

The mission of CLASP was to focus on creating active partnerships for communitywide literacy development. "Our schools cannot bear the full burden for developing reading skills in young people. Meeting this challenge requires the cooperation of parents, caregivers, teachers, community groups . . . and libraries." CLASP put this into practice through a series of programs creating new links among teachers, school and public librarians, and parents to encourage children's literacy development. One of the great strengths of CLASP was its community base, making partners of the city's public schools and branch libraries.[59]

The programs varied across communities and were designed to help create a full environment for literacy and reading by engaging school personnel and parents as well as students:

- A major outreach campaign to register all schoolchildren and their parents for library cards produced a new constituency of library users and readers.
- Class visits to libraries made librarians and libraries less intimidating places and encouraged students to come.
- Parent workshops to encourage involvement in student education gave parents assistance with reading to children and other literacy activities.
- Teacher workshops to improve channels of communication for educators allowed teachers to exchange ideas, share information, and give librarians advice.
- Family literacy programs highlighted the enjoyment of reading, as did summer reading programs and booklists.
- After-school programs for preschoolers, children, and teens used storytelling and reading aloud, providing alternatives to school-based learning.[60]

In the CLASP partnership, libraries spent time introducing young, middle-aged, and older patrons and students to CD-ROM databases, the

Internet, catalogs, and modern library resources. They also enhanced their book and materials collections to support school curricula, offered bilingual books to reflect the cultural makeup of the community, and provided multiple copies of school-assigned or core texts. Working with social service organizations, CLASP staff reached children and parents who might not be reached through usual school channels, such as youth at risk and mothers living in shelters. Collaborative projects were designed by library *and* school staff.

Since 1991, CLASP has dramatically altered the way New York City's branch libraries work with the schools and surrounding community. Parents, teachers, and children who had never set foot in their local public libraries became regular readers and library users. The library door has been opened wide to schoolteachers, students, and parents.

Two bicoastal examples, one from the Northeast and the other from the Northwest, illustrate community-based education and literacy development through technology collaborations. Technology permitted greater dissemination of information, literacy, and engagement of participants in educational activities across communities.

Going beyond structural collaboration and CBR are instances of libraries that seek community renewal. Consider Chicago's "Engaged Library," which includes literacy development but seeks community revitalization. The police conduct crime and safety workshops, and local residents contribute their ideas; day-care centers bring parents to the library; higher education institutions extend expert knowledge; senior citizens contribute their oral histories; schools support library academic programs; art and cultural institutions collaborate for creative projects; local businesses sponsor events; restaurants and cafés offer food; and faith-based organizations provide meeting space. This project, involving an extensive network of neighborhood branch libraries, designed a sophisticated asset-based framework to examine all aspects of community resources, included personnel (e.g., expertise, abilities, knowledge of community), facilities (e.g., for meetings and other activities), materials and equipment (e.g., books, computers, furniture, files, resources, information), economic power (e.g., job training, grant seeking), and networks of connections to private and public institutions.[61] All of these examples of transformative collaborations show that community literacy initiatives can take different forms, as they are adjusted to local and national circumstances, resources, and technology developments.

COMMUNITY-BASED EDUCATION GOALS

While libraries in the 19th century were expected to shadow schools and, in the 20th century, to become an extension of schools, especially with books, the tide may well be turning. Libraries are in good positions to provide an education *with* schools, especially through their rich multimodal resources— books, technology, and expertise—sharing all types of electronic resources and educational activities. The Gates Foundation, for example, gives to public libraries rather than school libraries because the former support lifelong learning to a range of publics, are open for longer hours, and are easily accessible. Moreover, public libraries are staffed by information professionals "whose mission it is—whatever the medium the information comes in—to help guide people to the resources they need."[62]

Libraries are currently viewed as valuable to community needs through information networking. A recent study for the American Councils for Libraries and the Bill and Melinda Gates Foundation found that the libraries hold high credibility in the public's eyes and across other community institutions. But more than this, they "serve communities as cultural and educational centers—as knowledge institutions—and by all accounts the public seems to expect them to go on doing so." Moreover, in cities that have experienced much downsizing of public services, libraries are renewing agencies, as they are "stable, welcoming, and modern" and are seen as communal property but not too associated with government.[63]

How can schools and libraries build and sustain enduring technology collaborations to contribute to communitywide literacy and civic engagement? Libraries cultivate an array of literacies that can get people to love reading and provide important skills for public engagement, work, home, community, and school. Schools focus on children's early literacy development and move to academic literacies, along with social and civic development. Libraries and schools together can use technology to widen access to lifelong learning opportunities, intensify engagement, diversify practices, and reinforce literacy acquisition through technology in communities by providing jointly different pathways. In this scenario, libraries and schools share their resources, expertise, and cultures—partnering to enhance literacy development while involving their communities in the process. These special projects and our case studies of libraries and schools suggest two major options for fruitful technology collaborations that emphasize learning as well as use, and extend the scope of "guardians of literacy" in communities.

Libraries and Schools as Holding Environments for Learning

Both libraries and schools are holding institutions in accepting young and old and confirming the importance of diverse literacies. They let go of students and patrons when they are ready to leave and stick around to provide continuity and change over time. Both schools and libraries have proven to be sturdy institutions with much public support and hold both electronic and print resources for public purposes. Learners can be supported in their literacy development at the first level by "being held" to develop technology literacy skills in library literacy programs or in schools and "let go" when people are ready to be challenged to learn more and different types of literacies. Even when they leave, they can always return to learn. Both institutions offer a safe stepping-stone into literacy development and, through their collaboration, can reengage learners time and again, as families and individuals.

Community-based organizations can support the transitions of learners through technology learning centers located in neighborhoods. Guidance counselors and school staff, librarians, and community technology center staff can help to connect learners to many different learning resources and ensure their persistence in learning. This process involves a concerted effort to engage in research, a strategy of action, and a plan with shared goals among a variety of community-based education partners.[64] They can be nested together, co-located, and even merged with one another—depending on the setting—adding a rich tapestry of community literacy while still maintaining their institutional identities because they are building on and expanding their strengths.

Libraries and Schools as Conduits for Learning

But libraries and schools can be more than holding institutions. They are agents for lifelong learning; even more, they are mediators for engaging communities in dialogue and new forms of expression via new technologies. They also act as information liaisons for helping people negotiate with other institutions, and they are advocates for community renewal.

Through effective community assessments and assistance, learners can transition from schools to libraries and back again—in a two-way street with constant traffic—to address their specific literacy needs and interests, at any given time, using technology to speed and enrich the process.

Libraries may be particularly suited to work with youth organizations in assisting teens in study and lifelong learning skills through tutor and peer mentoring programs using new technologies. They are launching pads for supplying a social network and instilling motivation in teens who disparage or despair of their school learning. Likewise, adults can be given referrals by schools and libraries to attend school district adult basic education offerings, community education, and library programs to learn as they improve their literacy rather than having to rely on only one program in a community. While adults may have done poorly at one time in school, they can go back to other adult education organizations for their various needs and interests. Human service agencies, ethnic associations, alcohol and drug recovery groups, and other community and charitable organizations, when they have the necessary financial support, can assist in the supply of additional services needed by adults and children to persist in returning to a learning setting.[65]

Together these institutions can launch community members into different kinds of learning, including group work and self-study. Study groups can be conversational and free-forming, while self-study can be initially structured and taught. New technologies can be used for various purposes, depending on the goals of the learners—even as drop-ins, supporting small, fluid communities of learning. Volunteer agencies, cultural organizations, family centers, senior organizations, and universities can support this development through virtual collaborations.

ENDURING INSTITUTIONS

Born of a similar mission but operating for decades as separated partners, schools and libraries have begun to move closer to one another in sharing scarce resources to advance literacy and enhance community life in recent years. We have offered many examples of urban and rural libraries and schools taking seriously collaboration of two core community institutions in privately and government-funded projects. Whether these special projects are examples of one-time efforts that will fade in time as staff efforts lag and dollars go elsewhere or whether these projects are early signs of an emerging partnership that will last beyond the next budget cycle—only time will tell. We would like to think it is the latter, but we are uncertain about the future when market forces seem to overpower public obligations to individuals and communities. For lifelong learning to be more than a bumper sticker slogan, the communities of literacy practices that evolve in families, workplaces, neighborhoods, and community agencies need to be spurred and sustained by public schools and libraries. That is a noble effort serving, enriching, and renewing both individuals and communities. It is a public good that needs public sustenance.

Notes

INTRODUCTION

1. Kozma & Shank, 1998, p. 5.
2. Interview notes of Sondra Cuban from three different studies in Hawai'i, North Carolina, California, and Washington, D.C.
3. Louise Blalock, personal correspondence with Sondra Cuban, December 6, 2005.
4. Interview notes of Sondra Cuban for Kathy Endaya, director of Project Read's Redwood City Public Library, as part of S. Cuban, 2003a, 2003b. See Porter, Cuban, & Comings, 2005.
5. George & Smoke, 1974; Skocpol & Sommers, 1980.
6. Kozma & Schank, 1998, p. 5; Barnett, 2003.
7. Hopey, 1998a; statistic on filters from Bertot, McClure, & Jaeger, 2005.
8. Warschauer, 2003.
9. Light, 2001.
10. Hettman, 2005, p. 11.
11. Brandt, 2005.
12. Grabill, 2001, p. 85.
13. Mossberger, Tolbert, & Stansbury, 2003.
14. Buschman, 2003, p. 37.
15. Bourke, 2005.
16. Barnett, 2003, p. 7.
17. Fellin, 1987; Galbraith, 1995.
18. Small & Supple, 2001, p. 162
19. Galbraith, 1995, p. 1.
20. Small & Supple, 2001.
21. Barrett, 2001.
22. Hamilton & Cunningham, 1989; Comer, Haynes, Joyner, & Ben-Avie, 1996.
23. The field of librarianship has developed ideas of community that fit within the adult education framework. For more information about how libraries conceptualize community, see, for example, de la Pena McCook, 2000; Monroe, 1979; Martin, 1989.

24. This ideal scenario is in Briscoe, 1990.

25. McKnight, 1987.

26. Humes, 1995.

27. The C-PALs website is www.c-pal.net

28. The website for this is http://ctcnet.org/who/network.htm; see also http://www.ed.gov/programs/comtechcenters/index.html

29. Puacz, 2005.

30. Kerka, 1997.

31. Adelman & Taylor, 1997.

32. Chaskin & Richman, 1992.

33. For projects to boost technology resources, see Henderson & Mapp, 2002.

34. Dryfoos, 1994; Comer, 1996; Riley, 2001; www.futureofchildren.org/information2827/information_show.htm?doc_id=71941-28k.

35. Barnett, 2003, pp. 53–54.

36. The cyberhood example is drawn from Warschauer, 2003, p. 167; see also Bohrer, 2004, pp. 311–312.

37. Gordon, 2004; Bertot, McClure, & Jaeger, 2005.

38. Bertot et al., 2005, p. 79.

39. Nunberg, 1998.

40. For diffusion theory, see Rogers, 1995. For institutional theory, see Meyer & Rowan, 1977; DiMaggio & Powell, 1960, pp. 147–160; Buschman, 2003.

41. Carter & Titzel, 2003; Ginsburg, 1998; Hayes, in press; Stites, 1998.

CHAPTER 1

1. *Good Schools Need Good Libraries*, n.d.

2. Quoted in Du Mont, 1977, p. 22.

3. Cremin, 1957, pp. 44, 77, 87.

4. Dewey, 1876, p. 5; Foster, 1879, p. 319.

5. Roszak, 1994, p. 197.

6. Cremin, 1957, p. 10.

7. For historical studies of these years, see Wiebe, 1967; Chandler, 1977; Cremin, 1988.

8. Adams, 1879, p. 334; Garrison, 1979.

9. Dain, 1975; Fain, 1983.

10. Du Mont, 1977, pp. 77–78.

11. Cremin, 1961; Tyack, 1974.

12. Heath, 1980.

13. The age-graded school, for example, influenced pedagogy. See Jackson, 1968.

14. Quoted in Molz & Dain, 1999, p. 206.

15. Dodge, 2005.

16. Garrison, 1979.

17. Lerner, 2002, p. 210.

18. Parker, 1997, chap. 3. For the pervasiveness of these outcome measures, see National Center for Education Statistics, 2005.

19. Quoted in Molz & Dain, 1999, p. 16.
20. Quoted ibid., pp. 16–17.
21. Patterson, 1986; Branch, 2006.
22. Patterson, 1996.
23. Ibid., pp. 769–770.
24. Ibid., pp. 455–457, 740–742.
25. National Commission on Excellence in Education, 1983.
26. Academic studies have concluded that for students to get middle-class wages in the labor market high school graduates would need at least a 9th-grade level of reading and math (hard skills) and such soft skills as communicating well with peers, both orally and in writing, solving semistructured problems, and working in groups with people of different backgrounds. Definitions of functional literacy, then, always changing in the late 20th century, followed deep shifts in the nation's economy and society. See Murnane & Levy, 1996. For a brief history of the movement toward standards-based reform with its accountability and testing, see Elmore, 2000.
27. For details of the formation of this market-inspired coalition concentrating on school reform, see Toch, 1991; Carnevale & Desrochers, 2003; Cuban, 2003. For a sequence of events in the same quarter-century whereby employers focused on workers' lack of skills and the need for more training and education to equip employees for the future workplace, see Lafer, 2002. Economists and widely respected analysts also produced bestsellers in these years that judged schools as failures at teaching students to think and solve problems. See Marshall & Tucker, 1992; Reich, 1991; and Thurow, 1992.
28. For more information, see Hursh, 2006.
29. "State of the Union Address," 2002.
30. Provisions of the law and current announcements can be found on the U.S. Department of Education's website devoted to NCLB: http://www.ed.gov/nclb/landing.jhtml?src=pb.
31. Public libraries extended their services to public schools during the early years of the progressive movement. John Cotton Dana, for example, as librarian for the Denver Public Library in 1889, lent books to teachers for classroom libraries. Years later, he served as secretary to the Denver Board of Education and later as president of the American Library Association. Eventually, Dana and an advocate for public libraries, Melvil Dewey, arranged for the National Education Association to begin a school library section in 1897. By 1915, school librarians had formed their own section of the ALA. School libraries, largely in high schools and later elementary schools as well, grew slowly through the 1950s. By 1954, nearly 40% of all U.S. schools had a school library, and by 2000, 92% had one. Moreover almost all the school libraries had a professional librarian, commonly a teacher who had taken professional courses in library studies and received a credential. By 2000, over 90% of school libraries had either been converted into media centers or contained a full array of electronic services. Because we are comparing public libraries and public schools in their espoused and actual mission as community institutions insofar as adopting new technologies is concerned, we do not address the specific role of school librarians working within the confines of the public school itself. See Pond, 1998; Michie & Holton, 2005.
32. Dodge, 2005.

33. Wiegand & Davis, 1994; Molz & Dain, 1999, pp. 8–9, 20.

34. Keilman, 2005; Lohr, 2004.

35. Molz & Dain, 1999, pp. 89–122.

36. Dodge, 2005.

37. Much of this section is adapted from L. Cuban, 2008. See also L. Cuban, 1986. For CAI, see Kulik, 1994, pp. 9–33; Tyack & Cuban, 1995, pp. 117–120; Oppenheimer, 2003, pp. 31–32, 116–117. For a vignette on an ILS in use in a Harlem school computer lab, see Oppenheimer, 2003, pp. 79–82.

38. Euchner, 1982; "Apple's Steve Jobs: 'Our Vision Is That We Have Just Begun,'" 2000.

39. "Technology Counts," 1998, pp. 7, 8; quote from high school principal in Oppenheimer, 2003, p. 10.

40. Quoted in Oppenheimer, 2003, pp. 143, 162, 167.

41. See http://www.ed.gov/TechnologyPlan/NatTechPlan/execsum.html

42. "Technology Counts," 1997, p. 8; "Pencils Down: Technology's Answer to Testing," 2003, p. 45. For use of computers in homes with children, see http://sacramento.bizjournals.com/sacramento/stories/2001/09/03/daily21.html

43. "Technology Counts," 2002, p. 54; *Survey Shows Widespread Enthusiasm for High Technology*, 2000.

44. American Library Association, 2005.

45. Quoted in Americans for Libraries Council, 2006.

46. American Library Association, 2002.

47. Ibid.

48. The Community Decency Act of 1996 is an amendment to the Telecommunication Act of 1996. For the court challenge and other details, see http://www.cybertelecom.org/cda/cda-up.htm; for the USA Patriot Act and its provisions for libraries, see http://www.ala.org

CHAPTER 2

1. Lagemann, 1989.

2. Institutionalization can be defined as "a developmental process that appears during and after the implementation of an innovation" (i.e., computers) and is "used in a routine manner and . . . accepted by the users as something normal that is expected to continue" (Elkhorn & Trier, 1987, quoted in Pickeral, 2002, p. 10).

3. Scott, 2005. For frameworks, see Bolman & Deal, 1984.

4. Kaestle, 1991.

5. Powell & Dimaggio, 1991, p. 66; See also Meyer & Scott, 1983.

6. The discussion of the early and middle time periods of libraries is drawn, with modifications from Lee, 1966. The discussion of the later period is drawn from Buschman, 2003, and Molz & Dain, 1999.

7. Buschman, 2003.

8. Harris & Hannah, 1992.

9. Van Fleet & Raber, 1990.

10. Benton Foundation, 1996. See http://www.benton.org/publibrary/kellogg/buildings.html

11. Wiegand, 1994.

12. Antin, 1969, p. 364; Gatto, n.d.; quote from Irving Stone, http://www .ifla.org/I/humour/subj.htm

13. Graff, 1991.

14. Ibid, p. 26.

15. Quoted in Harris, 1973, p. 2513; quoted in Learned, 1924, p. 70.

16. Budd, 1995, 2003.

17. Antin, 1969, p. 339; Wiegand, 1998; Harris, 1986, 1995.

18. Wiegand, 1998, p. 80; Harris, 1986.

19. Garrison, 1979; Radford, 1998; Van Fleet & Raber, 1990; Wiegand, 1998, p. 80; Lee, 1966, chapters on "Organizing Resources."

20. Dewey, 1898/1975. See http://juteux.net/rory/wbm7.html; Battles, 2003, pp. 150–151.

21. Quote from Dewey in Vann, 1978, p. 71; Van Slyck, 1995; Radway, 1994.

22. Van Slyck, 1995; Scott, 1991; Malone, 1994.

23. Dewey, 1876; Wiegand & Davis, 1994; Nunberg, 1998. See http://www .prospect.org/print/V9/41/nunberg-g.html

24. Chamberlain, 1895, p. 302.

25. Ibid., p. 300.

26. Dain, 1975.

27. Rose, 1917, p. 8.

28. Weigand, 1989; Lee, 1966; Borden, 1931; Nunberg, 1998, p. 17; Birge, 1981; Commission on the Library and Adult Education, 1926, p. 8.

29. Shera, 1965; Monroe,1963; Ranganathan, 1963.

30. Tyack, 1974; Tyack, Hansot, and Lowe, 1984.

31. Commission on the Library and Adult Education, 1926, p. 24.

32. Sources on Flexner and Wyer in Lee, 1966; Learned, 1924, p. 36.

33. Johnson, 1938; Birge, 1981; Monroe, 1963.

34. Birge, 1981.

35. Lee, 1966; de la Pena McCook & Barber, 2001; Berelson, 1949.

36. Lee, 1966, p. 85.

37. Lyman, 1954; Phinney, 1956; Lee, 1966.

38. PLA Guidelines are in Birge, 1981, p. 110.

39. Quote from Thomas Ballard in Rolstad, 1990, p. 251.

40. Lipsman, 1972, p. 432; McDonald, 1966.

41. Monroe, 1986, p. 200.

42. Birge, 1981, p. 114.

43. Graubard, 1972; Featherstone, 1971; Levin, 1970.

44. Ravitch, 1983; Tyack & Hansot, 1982.

45. Molz & Dain, 1999, p. 24.

46. L. Cuban, 1986.

47. Van Fleet & Raber, 1990; see also Van House, Lynch, McClure, Zweizig, & Rodger, 1987.

48. D'Elia, 1993.

49. Cronin, 1995; Anderson, 1998.

50. Kniffel, 1988; Symons & Stoffle, 1988, p. 56.

51. Fountain, 2001.

52. Buschman, 2003; Molz & Dain, 1999; Harris, 1986; Carbone, 1991.
53. Grubb & Lazerson, 2004; L. Cuban, 2008.
54. Dewey, 1916, p. 25; Tight, 2004.
55. Rachal, 1990.
56. Monroe, 1963; Cyril Houle argues for the role of the public library in adult education, quoting Lester Asheim in Chobot, 1989, pp. 369–383.
57. Chobot, 1989; Lyman, 1977a, 1977b.
58. Tight, 2004; Weigand, 1986, p. 188.
59. Chobot, 1989, p. 372.
60. Ibid.
61. Estabrook & Lakner, 2000.
62. "21st Century Literacy," 1998; McClure, 1994.
63. McClure, Bertot, & Zweizig, 1994; Buschman, 2003.
64. "Retooling Literacy for the 21st Century," 1998; McClure et al., 1994; McClure, 1994; Americans for Libraries Council, 2006.
65. Carter & Titzel, 2003; Main & Whittaker, 1991.
66. Barber, 1997, p. 42; for campaign, see "21st Century Literacy," 1998.
67. Rogers, 1995.
68. Dodge, 2005, p. 74.
69. Putnam, quoted in de la Pena McCook, 1997; Buschman, 2003, p. 113.
70. Hawai'i State Public Library System, 1991; Roszak, 1994; Buschman, 2003, p. 111.
71. Goodlad, 1984; Tyack & Cuban, 1995; Labaree, 1997; Cuban, L., 2001.
72. Broderick, 1997; Roszak, 1994, pp. 181, 197.
73. Roush, 2005; Roszak, 1994.
74. Hildebrand, 1997.
75. Pritchard, 1994, p. 45.
76. Harris, 1992.
77. Ibid., pp. 8, 11.
78. McClure, 1994, p. 122.
79. Gordon, 2004. See http://www.gatesfoundation.org/nr/Downloads/libraries/uslibraries/reports/TowardEqualityofAccess.pdf.

CHAPTER 3

1. Monroe, 1986.
2. Nauratil, 1985; Birge, 1981; Schmidt, 1978; Du Mont, 1977; Cook, 1977; Rolstad, 1990; Lipsman, 1972; de la Pena McCook, 1992; Mathews, Chute, & Cameron, 1986; Monroe, 1986; Lyman, 1977a; Salter and Salter, 1991; Zweizig, Robbins, and Johnson, 1988.
3. Lyman, 1977a, 1977b.
4. Zweizig et al., 1988; Smith, 1984; Quezada, 1992.
5. Main & Whittaker, 1991.
6. Kirsch, Jungeblatt, & Kolstad, 1992; see http://www.literacycampus.org/download/NALS.pdf for more information on the National Adult Literacy Survey; see http://nces.ed.gov/naal/ for the 2003 National Assessments of Adult Lit-

eracy (NAAL). For library literacy program studies, see Estabook & Lakner, 2000; Spangenberg, 1996; Main & Whittaker, 1991.

7. Martin, 2001; Main & Whittaker, 1991.

8. "Retooling Literacy for the 21st Century," 1998; "To Read, to Write, to Understand," 1997; Coleman, 1983.

9. Talan, 1990, p. 49; Kingery, 1990.

10. Main & Whittaker, 1991.

11. Ibid.

12. Quoted in Kerka, 1998.

13. Spangenberg, 1996.

14. S. Cuban, 1999.

15. Hawai'i State Public Library System, 1991b, pp. 8, 83; see also Hawai'i State Public Library System, 1991.

16. Reid, 1997; American Library Association, 1999. See also http://www.ala .org/Template.cfm?Section=outsourcing&Template=/ContentManagement/Content Display.cfm&ContentID=64971; *Hawaii Auditor Criticizes Kane* at http://www.ala .org/ala/alonline/currentnews/newsarchive/1998/january1998/hawaiiauditor.htm; Spires & Hill, n.d.

17. For statistics on Hawaii's assessments of literacy, see Omnitrak Research and Marketing Group, 1989. Quotation is from an untitled library report from Bartholomew Kane dated March 7, 1996, in S. Cuban, 1999.

18. Excerpt of "The Case for Computers" in S. Cuban, 1999, pp. 4–5.

19. Unpublished library literacy survey in S. Cuban, 1999.

20. For more information on technology and adult basic skills programs, see S. Cuban, 1999; Hopey, 1998.

21. Estabrook & Lakner, 2000, p. 13.

22. Spangenberg, 1996; S. Cuban, 1999; Zweizig et al., 1988; Estabrook & Lakner, 2000, p. 18.

23. Estabrook & Lakner, 2000, p. 44.

24. See "Overview" in Comings, Cuban, Bos, & Taylor, 2001; Comings & Cuban, 2000; Comings, Cuban, Bos, & Porter, 2003.

25. Ibid.

26. See Sumerford, 2001; http://www.ala.org/ala/olos/outreachresource/services newnonreaders.htm

27. Citron, n.d.

28. See also Comings et al., 2001; Comings & Cuban, 2000; Comings et al., 2003; Porter, Cuban, & Comings, 2005; S. Cuban, 2003a.

29. Sources for this analysis include S. Cuban's interview and field notes from 1999 through 2003 for the study reported in Porter, Cuban, & Comings, 2005.

30. Rosen, 2000.

31. Olgren, 2000; see also Imel, 2001, 2003.

32. Wonacott, 2001. See http://www.calpro-online.org/eric/docgen.asp?tbl= digests&ID=118

33. This quotation and subsequent quotes come from the author's notes of interviews with students, tutors, and staff in the library literacy programs previously mentioned in this section.

34. Ginsburg, 1998.

35. Imel, 2003; Olgren, 2000.
36. Nixon & Ponder, 2001.
37. O'Connor & Guerra, 2001.
38. Imel, 2001.
39. Citron, n.d.

CHAPTER 4

1. "Pencils Down: Technology's Answer to Testing," 2003, p. 45; Trotter et al., 1997.
2. L. Cuban, 1986.
3. For a typical example, see *Educational Environment for the Future*, 2001.
4. Faux, 1997, p. 29.
5. Friedman, 2006.
6. See Consortium on Productivity in the Schools, 1995. Gerstner speech to National Governors' Conference of 1995, cited in Glennan & Melmed, 1996, p. 9.
7. For a typical example of articles touting laptops, see Public Policy Institute of New York State, 2003. Nicolas Negroponte of MIT has developed a $100 computer for poor children in developing nations. See http://www.boston.com/news/education/higher/articles/2005/09/28/for_each_poor_child_in_world_a_laptop/
8. President's Committee of Advisors on Science and Technology, Panel on Educational Technology, 1997, p. 33. See also Dede, 1990; Means, 1995; Sandholtz, Ringstaff, & Dwyer, 1997.
9. Archer & Walsh, 1996, pp. 12, 15. Policy statement text is on p. 13.
10. For recent demographics and statistics on the digital divide, see the National Telecommunications and Information Administration reports at http://www.ntia.doc.gov/reports/anol/index.html
11. Light, 2001.
12. The fear of a digital divide that swept across the media and stirred policymakers and business leaders in the early 1990s dissolved within a few years as access to computers climbed among low-income families and access to computers in schools became widespread. That fear joined a concern for the poor with an unvarnished faith in the power of computers to "solve" the problem of poverty, another excursion into using schools to cope with larger economic problems. See Trotter, 2003, p. 9; Samuelson, 2002.
13. Becker & Ravitz, 2001; Cuban, Kirkpatrick, & Peck, 2001. See "Technology Counts (student perspective)," 1999.
14. L. Cuban, 2005. The author makes the point that the thousand-plus reports of lessons collected included over 350 observations of classrooms that principals and other supervisors made and over 160 that Cuban directly observed. In most of these observations, the administrator or supervisor was in the classroom from 10 to 20 minutes, which is why these are called snapshots of lessons. Most research on classroom use of ICT is conducted through surveys of teachers, principals, and supervisors, producing results that are, at best, self-reports of participants or perceptions of what goes on in classrooms.

15. There are rigorous multimethod studies, including classroom observations, where teachers who have gone through a carefully planned and locally relevant professional development increased their daily use of ICT and integrated the technologies into their daily lessons. See Sandholtz & Kelly, 2004. Also see a description of the federally funded Berkeley (California) elementary and middle school program called Teacher Led Technology Challenge Project, where site-based professional development and technical support resulted in sharply increased classroom use of technology by teachers over 5 years in L. Cuban, 2001, pp. 184–188.

16. Papert, 1980; Sandholtz et al., 1997; L. Cuban et al., 2001.

17. Sandholtz et al., 1997.

18. Ibid., p. 6.

19. On the stages of entry, adoption, adaptation, appropriation, and invention, see ibid., pp. 52–53.

20. Kirkpatrick & Cuban, 1998a. See http://www.ait.net/technos/tq_07/2cuban.php; Kulik & Kulik, 1991.

21. Clark & Feldon, 2005. For research on writing improvements as a result of student use of computers, see Kulik, 2003.

22. Curtis, 2003; Barton, 2003.

23. Clark, 1983, 1991; Schramm, 1977.

24. Fuchs & Woessmann, 2004. A critique of this study that points out the correlations and the stir that the economists' study created can be found in Bielefeldt, 2005.

25. For a particularly rigorous statistical design studying laptop use of cohorts of students over time in a California district that fails to separate instructional methods from the presence of laptops, see Gulek & Demirtas, 2005.

26. Education Development Center and SRI International, 2004; Rockman, 2003; Silvernail & Lane, 2004.

27. Hook & Rosenshine, 1979; Mayer, 1999; Viadero, 2005.

28. *1 to 1 Learning*, 2006.

CHAPTER 5

1. de la Pena McCook, 2000, p. 1.

2. Americans for Libraries Council, 2006, p. 68.

3. Levey, 2005.

4. Kretzmann & Rans, 2006.

5. Barnett, 2003, p. 47.

6. Putnam & Feldstein, 2003. While we do support locally grown initiatives, we do not discount the importance of federal and state financial and infrastructural support. The point is that the community programs should be informed, designed, and disseminated at a communitywide level.

7. Barton & Hamilton, 1998; Barton, 1994; Street, 1984; Lankshear & Knobel, 2004; Brandt, 2001.

8. Brandt & Clinton, 2002; Lankshear & Knobel, 2004; Barton & Hamilton, 2005.

9. Ward & Watson-Ellam, 2005; Street, 1984.

10. Ibid.; Barton, Hamilton, & Ivanivic, 2000; Lankshear & Knobel, 2004; Gee, 2003.

11. For the list of literacies, we draw on Hull, Mikulecky, St. Clair, & Kerka, 2003.

12. This school is now called the Highlander Research and Education Center. More information about what they do can be found on their website (http://www.highlandercenter.org/). See also Horton, Kohl, & Kohl, 1998.

13. For a definition of environmental literacy, see Hull, Mikulecky, St. Clair, & Kerka, 2003.

14. For a definition of health literacy, see ibid.

15. Lankshear & Knobel, 2004. See also Lankshear, Snyder, & Gree, 2000.

16. Bruce, 1996.

17. O'Neil, 2004.

18. American Library Association, 2006a, 2006b; see also Crowther & Trott, 2004.

19. Resnick & Glennan, 2002.

20. Kronkosky Charitable Foundation, 2005.

21. Gordon, 2004; Bell et al. in Kronkosky Charitable Foundation, 2005.

22. Hueretz, Gordon, & Gordon, 2003.

23. For more on this project, see http://webjunction.org/do/DisplayContent?id=1232

24. Hueretz et al., 2003; Lewis, Farris, & Westat, 2002.

25. Lenhart, Madden, & Hitlin, 2005; Gordon, 2004.

26. Bill and Melinda Gates Foundation, 2006; Gordon, Gordon, Moore, & Boyd, 2002; Yohalem & Pittman, 2003; *Public Libraries as Partners in Youth Development*, 1999.

27. Ward & Watson-Ellam, 2005; Lankshear & Knobel, 2004.

28. *Public Libraries as Partners in Youth Development*, 1999.

29. Lo, 2005, p. 6.

30. Yohalem & Pittman, 2003, p. 12; Spielberger, Horton, & Michaels, 2004.

31. Kronkosky Charitable Foundation, 2005; Shriver, 2002. See also Benoit, 2004; Lewis et al., 2002.

32. Sumerford, personal conversation, October 12, 2005. See also Whiteside, 2004; Gordon, 2004.

33. Bose, 2005.

34. This applies to patrons and librarians alike. Garrison, 1979; Berelson, 1949; Estabrook, 1997.

35. Warschauer, 2003, p. 55; Kirkpatrick & Cuban, 1998b.

36. Kirkpatrick & Cuban, 1998b.

37. Walter, Mediavilla, Braun, & Meyers, 2005.

38. Williams, Burgess, Bray, Bransford, Goldman, & Cognition and Technology Group at Vanderbilt, 1998.

39. Hayes, 2000; "Youth in ABA," 2004.

40. Yohalem & Pittman, 2003.

41. Yohalem & Pittman, 2003; Spielberger, Horton, & Michaels, 2004. See also *Connecting Learners to Libraries*, n.d.

42. Afterschool Alliance, n.d.

43. For 21st century community learning centers, see U.S. Department of Education website: http://www.ed.gov/programs/21stcclc/index.html; http://www.ed.gov/pubs/After_School_Programs/Technology_Programs.html

44. Warschauer, 2003.

45. Gee, 2001; Heath, 1983; Anyon, 1980. While Anyon's study focused on social class differences—both schools were largely White—the literature on Black and Hispanic schools where teachers engage in largely rote activities with students is ample. See Rosenfeld, 1971. For teachers who reported what other teachers did and how they tried to teach differently, see Kohl, 1967; Herndon, 1997. See also Mathews, 1988.

46. See various articles by Stanley Pogrow and general information on HOTS at http://www.hots.org/articles.html

47. Estabrook & Lakner, 2000; Kretzmann & Rans, 2006. For more information on Project READ, see Porter, Cuban, & Comings, 2005.

48. Hayes, in press; Gee, 2003; Squire & Stenkeuhler, 2005.

49. Squire & Stenkeuhler, 2005; Lipschultz, 2005.

50. de la Pena McCook, 2004; Bruner, 1991; Cranton, 2006.

51. Witherell & Noddings, 1990, p. 1.

52. Fanning, 1995; Bruner, 1990.

53. Bruner, 1990

54. Kerka, 1997.

55. Kerka, 1997. See also Karasoff, 1998.

56. Strand, Murullo, Cutforth, Stoecker, & Donohue, 2003.

57. Ibid.

58. See SCTA information at: http://www.ci.seattle.wa.us/Tech/overview/default.htm; *Connecting Learners to Libraries*, n.d.

59. Delvechio, 1993. CLASP was a long-running project, starting in 1991 and ending in 2005–06.

60. Ibid.

61. Kretzmann & Rans, 2006.

62. Molz & Dain, 1999, p. 205.

63. Americans for Libraries Council, 2006; Molz & Dain, 1999, pp. 193, 205.

64. For holding environments, see Kegan, Broderick, Drago-Severson, Helsing, Popp, & Portnow, 2006; Americans for Libraries Council, 2006.

65. The different types of organizations are drawn from Kretzman & Rans, 2006; S. Cuban, 2003b.

References

Adams, C. F. (1870). Fiction in public libraries and educational catalogues. *Library Journal, 4*(9), 330–338.

Adelman, H., & Taylor, L. (1997). Addressing barriers to learning: Beyond school-linked services and full-service schools. *American Journal of Orthopsychiatry, 67*(3), 408–421.

Afterschool Alliance. (n.d.). *America after 3 p.m.: A household survey on after-school in America: Key findings.* Retrieved January 16, 2007, from www.afterschool alliance.org

American Library Association. (1999). *Outsourcing and privatization in American libraries: Report of the ALA outsourcing task force.* Chicago: Author.

American Library Association. (2002). *Public information office press kit.* Retrieved January 16, 2007, from http://www.ala.org/ala/pio/piopresskits/placonference/librariesdigital.htm

American Library Association. (2005). *Interface, 27*(3).

American Library Association. (2006a). *Building a community of readers through partnerships and technology.* Retrieved January 16, 2007, from http://www.ala.org/ala/olos/outreachresource/servicesnewnonreaders.htm

American Library Association. (2006b). *Services to adult new and non-readers.* Retrieved January 14, 2007, from http://www.ala.org/ala/olos/outreachresource/servicesnewnonreaders.htm

Americans for Libraries Council. (2006). *Americans for libraries: Long overdue: A fresh look at public attitudes about libraries in the 21st century.* Retrieved January 14, 2007, from http://www.lff.org/long_overdue061306.html

Anderson, J. (2006, March 23). *Filling in the achievement gap with hard work, strict laws, and more funding* [HGSE News Features and Releases]. Retrieved January 16, 2007, from http://www.gse.harvard.edu/news_events/features/2006/03/23_abbott.html

Anderson, P. M. (1998). Bookstore backlash: Wow did we get letters! *American Libraries, 29*(5), 76.

Antin, M. (1969). *The promised land.* Boston: Houghton-Mifflin.

Anyon, J. (1980). Social class and the hidden curriculum of work. *Journal of Education, 162*(3), 67–74.

Apple Computers. (2006, February 20). *1 to 1 learning: A review and analysis by the Metiri Group*. Retrieved January 16, 2007, from http://www.apple.com/education/k12/onetoone

Apple's Steve Jobs.: "Our vision is that we have just begun." (2000, September 25). *Business Week Online*. Retrieved January 16, 2007, from http://www.businessweek.com/2000/00_39/b3700122.htm

Archer, J., & Walsh, M. (1996, April 3). Summit garners mixed reviews from pundits, practitioners. *Education Week*, p. 12.

Baker. E., & O'Neill, H. (Eds.). (1994). *Technology assessment in education and training*. Hillsdale, NJ: Erlbaum.

Barber, P. (1997). Computers, technology, books—but literacy must come first. *American Libraries, 26*(5), 42.

Barrett, A. L. (2001). Taking neighborhoods seriously. In A. Booth & A. Crouter (Eds.), *Does it take a village? Community effects on children, adolescents, and families* (pp. 31–47). Mahwah, NJ: Erlbaum.

Barnett, A. (2003). *Libraries, community, and technology*. Jefferson, NC: McFarland.

Barton, D. (1994). *Literacy: An introduction to the ecology of written language*. Oxford, UK: Blackwell.

Barton, D., & Hamilton, M. (1998). *Local literacies: Reading and writing in one community*. London: Routledge.

Barton, D., & Hamilton, M. (2005). Literacy, reification, and the dynamics of social interaction. In D. Barton & K. Tusting (Eds.), *Beyond communities of practice: Language, power, and social context* (pp. 14–35). New York: Cambridge University Press.

Barton, D., Hamilton, M., & Ivanivic, R. (Eds.). (2000). *Situated literacies: Reading and writing in context*. London: Routledge.

Barton, D., & Tusting, K. (Eds.). (2005). *Beyond communities of practice: Language, power, and social context*. New York: Cambridge University Press.

Barton, R. (2003, Winter). In the Chugach district, the sky is the limit. *Northwest Education Magazine, 9*(2), 20. Retrieved January 16, 2007, from http://www.nwrel.org/nwedu/09–02/chugach.asp

Battles, M. (2003). *Library: An unquiet history*. New York: Norton.

Becker, H., & Ravitz, J. (2001, March). *Computer use by teachers: Are Cuban's predictions correct?* Paper presented at the annual meeting of the American Educational Research Association, Seattle.

Benoit, H. (2004). Family language kit program: Connecting with immigrant families. In R. Osborne & S. Orange (Eds.), *From outreach to equity: Innovative models of library policy and practice*. Chicago: America Library Association. Retrieved January 16, 2007, from http://www.webjunction.org/do/DisplayContent?id=2478

Benton Foundation. (1996). *Buildings, books, and bytes: Perspectives on the Benton Foundation report on libraries in the digital age*. Washington, DC: Author.

Berelson, B. (1949). *The library's public: A report of the public library inquiry*. New York: Columbia University Press.

Bertot, J. C., McClure, C., & Jaeger, P. T. (2005). Public libraries struggle to meet internet demand. *American Libraries, 36*(7), 78–79.

Bielefeldt, T. (2005). Computers and student learning: Interpreting the multivariate analysis of PISA 2000. *Journal of Research in Technology, 37*(3). Retrieved January 16, 2007, from http://eric.ed.gov/ERICWebPortal/Home.portal?_nfpb= true&_pageLabel=RecordDetails&ERICExtSearch_Search Value_0=EJ690976 &ERICExtSearch_SearchType_0=eric_accno&objectId=0900000b802bd182

Bill and Melinda Gates Foundation. (2006). *U.S. library program: Summary of research reports.* Retrieved January 16, 2007, from http://www.gatesfoundation .org/Libraries/USLibraryProgram/Evaluation/default.htm

Birge, L. E. (1981). *Serving adult learners.* Chicago: American Library Association.

Bohrer, C. N. (2004, November/December). Libraries at risk? *Public Libraries, 43*(6), p. 311.

Bolman, L. E., & Deal, T. (1984). *Modern approaches to understanding and managing organizations.* San Francisco: Jossey-Bass.

Booth, A., & Crouter, A. (Eds.). (2001). *Does it take a village? Community effects on children, adolescents, and families.* Mahwah, NJ: Erlbaum.

Borden, A. (1931, January). The sociological beginnings of the library movement. *Library Quarterly, 1,* 279–282.

Bose, A. (2005). Online activism for women's rights and civic participation. *Visible Minority Women and ICTs-MOIVMWC* [Fact sheets]. Retrieved January 14, 2007, from http://www.womenspace.ca/policy/facts_minority.html

Bourke, C. (2005). Public libraries: Building social capital through networking. *APLIS, 18*(2), 71–75.

Branch, T. (2006). *At Canaan's edge.* New York: Simon & Schuster.

Brandt, D. (2001). *Literacy in American lives.* New York: Cambridge University Press.

Brandt, D. (2005). Writing for a living: Literacy and the knowledge economy. *Written Communication, 22*(2), 166–197.

Brandt, D., & Clinton, K. (2002). Limits of the local: Expanding perspectives on literacy as a social practice. *Journal of Literacy Research, 34*(3), 337–356.

Briscoe, D. B. (1990). Community-education: A culturally responsive approach to learning. In J. M. Ross-Gordon, L. Martin, & D. Briscoe (Eds.), *New directions for adult and continuing education, No. 48: Serving culturally diverse populations* (pp. 81–91). San Francisco: Jossey-Bass.

Broderick, D. (1997, July). Turning library into a dirty word: A rant. *Library Journal,* pp. 42–43.

Bruce, B. C. (1996). Technology as social practice. *Educational Foundations, 10*(4), 51–58.

Bruner, J. (1990). *Acts of meaning.* Cambridge, MA: Harvard University Press.

Bruner, J. (1991). The narrative construction of reality. *Critical Inquiry, 18*(1), 1–21.

Budd, J. (1995). An epistemological foundation for library and information science. *Library Quarterly, 65*(3), 295–318.

Budd, J. (2003). The library, praxis, and symbolic power. *Library Quarterly, 73*(1), 19–32.

Burge, E. J. (2000). *The strategic use of learning technologies: New directions for adult and continuing education.* San Francisco: Jossey-Bass.

Buschman, J. (2003). *Dismantling the public sphere: Situating and sustaining librarianship in the age of the new public philosophy.* Westport, CT: Libraries Unlimited.

Carbone, M. (1991). A critical inquiry into librarianship: Applications of the new sociology of education. *Library Quarterly, 61,* 15–30.

Carnevale, A., & Desrochers, D. (2003). *Standards for what? The economic roots of K–16 reform.* Princeton, NJ: Educational Testing Service.

Carter, J., & Titzel, J. (2003). *Technology in today's ABE classroom.* Boston: World Education.

Chamberlain, M. (1879). Public library and public school. *Library Journal, 5*(11/12), 300–302.

Chandler, A., Jr. (1977). *The visible hand: The managerial revolution in American business.* Cambridge, MA: Harvard University Press.

Chaskin, R. J., & Richman, H. A. (1992). Concerns about school-linked services: Institution-based versus community-based models. *The future of children: School-linked services, 2*(1), 107–117.

Chobot, M. C. (1989). Public libraries and museums. In S. Merriam & P. Cunningham (Eds.), *Handbook of adult and continuing education* (pp. 369–383). San Francisco: Jossey-Bass.

Citron, A. (n.d.). Unpublished, untitled paper on computers, technology, and library literacy programs.

Clark, R. (1983). Reconsidering research on media in learning. *Review of Educational Research, 53*(4), 445–460.

Clark, R. (1991, February). When researchers swim upstream: Reflections on an unpopular argument about learning from media. *Educational Technology,* pp. 34–40.

Clark, R., & Feldon, D. (2005). Five common but questionable principles of multimedia learning. In R. Mayer (Ed.), *The Cambridge handbook of multimedia learning* (pp. 97–115). New York: Cambridge University Press.

Coleman, J. E. (1983). The social responsibilities of librarians toward literacy education. In Patricia Schuman (Ed.), *Social responsibilities of librarians* (pp. 31–40). New York: Bowker.

Comer, J. P., Haynes, N. M., Joyner, E. T., & Ben-Avie, M. (1996). *Rallying the whole village: The Comer process of reforming education.* New York: Teachers College Press.

Comings, J., & Cuban, S. (2000). *So I made up my mind: Introducing a study of adult learner persistence in library literacy programs.* New York: Wallace Foundation.

Comings, J., Cuban, S., Bos, J., & Porter, K. (2003). *As long as it takes: Responding to the challenges of adult student persistence in library literacy programs.* New York: MDRC.

Comings, J., Cuban, S., Bos, J., & Taylor, C. J. (2001, September). *I did it for myself: Studying efforts to increase adult student persistence in library literacy programs.* New York: MDRC.

Comings, J., Garner, B., & Smith, C. (2000). *The annual review of adult learning and literacy.* San Francisco: Jossey-Bass.

Commission on the Library and Adult Education. (1926). *Libraries and adult education.* New York: American Library Association and Macmillan.

Connecting learners to libraries [Washington State Library Project]. (n.d.). Retrieved January 21, 2007, from http://www.secstate.wa.gov/library/libraries/projects/connecting/

Consortium on Productivity in the Schools. (1995). *Using what we have to get the schools we need: A productivity focus for American education.* New York: Author.

Cook, W. D. (1977). *Adult literacy education in the United States.* Newark, DE: International Reading Association.

Cranton, P. (2006). *Understanding and promoting transformative learning: A guide for educators of adults.* San Francisco: Jossey-Bass.

Cremin, L. (Ed.). (1957). *The republic and the school: Horace Mann on the education of free men.* New York: Teachers College Press.

Cremin, L. (1961). *The transformation of the school.* New York: Vintage.

Cremin, L. (1988). *American education: The metropolitan experience, 1876–1980.* New York: Harper & Row.

Cronin, B. (1995). Shibboleth and substance in North American library and information science education. *Libri, 45*(1), 45–63.

Crowther, J., & Trott, B. (2004). *Partnering with purpose.* Denver: Libraries Unlimited.

Cuban, L. (1986). *Teachers and machines: The classroom use of technology since 1920.* New York: Teachers College Press.

Cuban, L. (2001). *Oversold and underused: Computers in the classroom.* Cambridge, MA: Harvard University Press.

Cuban, L. (2003). *Why is it so hard to get good schools?* New York: Teachers College Press.

Cuban, L. (2005). *Teaching in an era of testing and accountability, 1980–2005.* Unpublished report to the Spencer Foundation, Chicago.

Cuban, L. (2008). *The blackboard and the bottom line: Why schools can't be businesses.* Cambridge, MA: Harvard University Press.

Cuban, L., Kirkpatrick, H., & Peck, C. (2001). High access and low use of technologies in high school classrooms. *American Educational Research Journal, 38*(4), 813–834.

Cuban, S. (1999). *Before days: Women in a library literacy program in Hilo, Hawai'i talk story.* Unpublished doctoral dissertation. Madison: University of Wisconsin–Madison.

Cuban, S. (2003a, April). *Looking for another link: Building student persistence in programs and communities.* Paper presented at the annual meeting of the American Educational Research Association, Chicago.

Cuban, S. (2003b, April). *Libraries as literacy education brokers: The unique roles for library literacy programs within the adult education and literacy system.* Paper presented at the annual meeting of the American Educational Research Association, Chicago.

Curtis, D. (2003, January 24). A remarkable transformation. *Edutopia,* pp. 1–3.

Dain, P. (1975). Ambivalence and paradox: The social bonds of the public library. *Library Journal, 100,* 261–266.

de la Pena McCook, K. (1992). Where would we be without them? Libraries and adult education activities, 1966–1991. *Reference and User Services Quarterly, 32*(12), 245–253.

de la Pena McCook, K. (1997). Search for new metaphors. *Library Trends, 46*(1).

de la Pena McCook, K. (2000). *A place at the table: Participating in community building.* Chicago: American Library Association.

de la Pena McCook, K. (2004). Cultural heritage institutions and community building. *Reference and User Services Quarterly, 41*(4), 326–329.

de la Pena McCook, K., & Barber, P. (2001). *Public policy as a factor influencing
adult lifelong learning, adult literacy and public libraries.* Retrieved on January 16, 2007, from http://www.cas.usf.edu/lis/literacy.htm

Decandido, G. A. (Ed.). (2001). *Literacy and libraries: Learning from case studies.*
Chicago: American Library Association.

Dede, C. J. (1990). *Imaging technology's role in restructuring for learning with technology.* New York: Center for Technology in Education, Bank Street College
of Education.

Dede, C. (Ed.). (1998). *Learning with technology.* Alexandria, VA: Association for
Supervision and Curriculum Development.

D'Elia, G. (1993). *The roles of the public library in society: The results of the national survey: Final report.* Evanston, IL: Urban Libraries Council.

Delvechio, S. (1993). Connecting libraries and schools with CLASP. *Wilson Library
Bulletin, 68*(1), 38–40.

Dewey, J. (1916). *Democracy and education. An introduction to the philosophy of
education.* New York: Free Press.

Dewey, M. (1876). The profession. *American Library Journal, 1,* 5.

Dewey, M. (1975). Relation of state to public library. In B. McCrimmon (Ed.),
American library philosophy: An anthology. Hamden, CT: Shoe String Press.
(Original work published 1898)

Dewitt-Wallace Readers Digest Fund. (1999). *Public libraries as partners in youth development.* New York: Author. Retrieved January 14, 2007, from www.wallace
foundation.org/ . . . /0/PublicLibrariesasPartnersinYouthDevelopment.pdf

DiMaggio, P., & Powell, W. W. (1960). The iron cage revisited: Institutional isomorphism and collective rationality in organizational fields. *American Sociological Review, 48,* 147–160.

Dodge, C. (2005, July/August). Knowledge for sale. *Utne Reader,* pp. 73–77. Retrieved January 14, 2007, from http://www.utne.com/pub/2005_130/promo/
11706-html

Dryfoos, J. G. (1994). *Full-service schools: A revolution in health and social services for children, youth, and family.* San Francisco: Jossey-Bass.

Du Mont, R. (1977). *Reform and reaction: The big city public library in American
life.* Westport, CT: Greenwood Press.

Educational environment for the future. (2001). Retrieved January 14, 2007, from
http://ed.fnal.gov/lincon/w01/projects/futureschool/scenarioBh.htm

Education Development Center and SRI international. (2004, June). *New study of
large-scale district laptop initiative shows benefits of "one-to-one computing."*
Retrieved January 21, 2007, from http://main.edc.org/newsroom/Features/
edc_sri.asp

Elmore, R. (2000). *Building a new structure for school leadership.* Washington, DC:
Albert Shanker Institute.

Estabrook, L. (1997, February 1). Polarized perceptions. *Library Journal,* pp. 46–49.

Estabrook, L., & Lakner, E. (2000). *Literacy programs for adults in public libraries:
A survey report.* Champaign: University of Illinois, Library Research Center,
Graduate School of Library and Information Science.

Euchner, C. (1982, November 24). Passage of "Apple Bill" sought by E.D. and computer firm. *Education Week*, 2(12), 10, 14.

Fain, E. (1983). Books for new citizens: Public libraries and Americanization programs, 1900–1925. In R. M. Aderman (Ed.), *The quest for social justice II: The Morris Fromkin memorial lectures, 1981–1990* (pp. 255–276). Milwaukee: Golda Meier Library, University of Wisconsin–Milwaukee.

Fanning, J. (1995). *Rural school consolidation and student learning.* Retrieved January 21, 2007, from http://www.findarticles.com/p/articles/mi_pric/is_199508/ai_605590243. (ERIC No. ED 3844)

Faux, J. (1997, November/December). Can liberals tell a credible story? *American Prospect*, p. 29.

Featherstone, J. (1971). *Schools where children learn.* New York: Norton.

Fellin, P. (1987). *The community and the social worker.* Itasca, IL: Peacock.

Foster, W. E. (1879). The school and the library: Their mutual relation. *Library Journal*, 4(9), 319–325.

Fountain, J. (2001, August 23). Librarians adjust image in an effort to fill jobs. *New York Times*, p. A12.

Friedman, T. (2006, March 24). Worried about India's and China's booms? So are they. *New York Times*, pp. 1–2.

Fuchs, T., & Woessmann, L. (2004). *Computers and student learning: Bivariate and multivariate evidence on the availability and use of computers at home and school* (Ifo Institute for Economic Research, Working paper No. 1321). University of Munich, Germany. Retrieved January 21, 2007, from http://www.cesifo.de/DocCIDL/1321.pdf

Galbraith, M. (1995, April 19). *Community-based organizations and the delivery of lifelong learning opportunities.* Paper commissioned for the National Institute of Post-Secondary Education, Libraries and Museums, Washington, DC.

Garrison, D. (1979). *Apostles of culture: The public librarian and American society, 1876–1920.* New York: Free Press.

Gatto, J. T. (n.d.). *Confederacy of dunces: The tyranny of compulsory schooling.* Retrieved January 14, 2007, from http://www.spinninglobe.net/condunces.htm

Gee, J. P. (2001). Reading, language abilities, and semiotic resources: Beyond limited perspectives on reading. In J. Larson (Ed.), *Literacy as snake oil* (pp. 7–26). New York: Peter Lang.

Gee, J. P. (2003). *What videogames have to teach us about learning and literacy.* New York: Palgrave MacMillan.

George, A., & Smoke, R. (1974). Case studies and theory development: The method of structured, focused comparison. In P. Lauren (Ed.), *Diplomacy: New approaches in history, theory and policy* (pp. 43–68). New York: Free Press.

Ginsburg, L. (1998). Integrating technology into adult learning. In Chris Hopey (Ed.), *Technology, basic skills, and adult education* (pp. 37–45; ERIC series no. 372). Columbus, OH: ERIC.

Glennan, T., & Melmed, A. (1996). *Fostering the use of educational technology.* Santa Monica, CA: Rand.

Goodlad, J. I. (1984). *A place called school.* New York: McGraw-Hill.

Good schools need good libraries. (n.d.). Flyer printed by the Brooklyn Public Library, the New York Public Library, and Queens Public Library.

Gordon, A. (2004). *Toward equality of access: The role of public libraries in addressing the digital divide.* Seattle, WA: Gates Foundation.

Gordon, A. C., Gordon, M. T., Moore, E., & Boyd, A. (2002). *Support for public access computing widespread and strong.* Seattle, WA: Gates Foundation. Retrieved January 14, 2007, from www.gatesfoundation.org/NR/Downloads/

Grabill, J. T. (2001). *Community literacy programs and the politics of change.* Albany: State University of New York Press.

Graff, H. (1991, Winter). Literacy, libraries, and lives: New social and cultural histories. *Libraries and Culture, 6*(1), 24–45.

Graubard, A. (1972). *Free the children.* New York: Pantheon.

Grubb, N., & Lazerson, L. (2004). *The education gospel.* Cambridge, MA: Harvard University Press.

Gulek, J., & Demirtas, H. (2005). Learning with technology: The impact of laptop use on student achievement. *Journal of Technology, Learning, and Assessment, 3*(2), 3–38.

Hamilton, E., & Cunningham, P. M. (1989). Community-based adult education. In S. Merriam & P. Cunningham (Eds.), *Handbook of adult and continuing education* (pp. 439–450). San Francisco: Jossey-Bass.

Harris, M. (1973, September 15). Purpose of the American public library: A revisionist interpretation. *Library Journal, 98,* 2513.

Harris, M. (1986). State, class, and cultural reproduction: Toward a theory of library service in the United States. In W. Simonton (Ed.), *Advances in Librarianship, 14,* 211–252.

Harris, M. (1995). The fall of the grand hotel: Class, canon, and the coming crisis of Western librarianship. *Libri, 43,* 231–235.

Harris, M., & Hannah, S. (1992). Why do we study the history of libraries? *LISR, 14,* 123–130.

Harris, R. (1992, January). Information technology and deskilling of librarians. *Computers in Libraries,* pp. 9–16.

Hawai'i auditor criticizes Kane. (1998). *American Libraries Online.* Retrieved January 21, 2007, from http://www.ala.org/ala/alonline/currentnews/newsarchive/1998/january1998/hawaiiauditor.htm

Hawai'i State Public Library System. (1991a). *Affirmative action plan.* Honolulu: Author.

Hawai'i State Public Library System. (1991b). *Customer satisfaction: A master plan for public librarians.* Honolulu: Author.

Hawai'i State Public Library System. (1991c). *Report.* Honolulu: Author.

Hayes, E. (2000). Youth in adult literacy programs. In J. Comings, B. Garber, & C. Smith (Eds.), *The annual review of adult learning and literacy* (pp. 74–110). San Francisco, Jossey-Bass.

Hayes, E. (2005). Women, videogaming & learning: Beyond stereotypes. *TechTrends, 49*(5), 23–28.

Hayes, E. (in press). Reconceptualizing the digital divide. In A. Belzer & H. Beder (Eds.), *Defining and improving quality in adult education: Issues and challenges.* New York: Erlbaum.

Heath, S. B. (1980). The functions and uses of literacy. *Journal of Communication, 30*(2), 123–133.

Heath, S. B. (1983). *Ways with words.* New York: Cambridge University Press.

Heim, K., & Wallace, D. (Eds.). (1990). *Adult services: An enduring focus for public libraries.* Chicago: American Library Association.

Henderson, A. T., & Mapp, K. L. (2002). *New wave of evidence: The impact of school, family, and community connections on student achievement—National Center for Family and Community Connections with Schools.* Austin, TX: Southwest Educational Development Laboratory.

Herndon, J. (1997). *Way it spozed to be.* Portsmouth, NH: Boynton/Cook.

Hettman, E. (2005, August 15). Conference: Secretary of Labor addresses need to compete globally. *Community College Week.*

Hightower, A. M., Knapp, M. S., Marsh, J. A., & McLaughlin, M. W. (Eds.). (2002). *School districts and instructional renewal.* New York: Teachers College Press.

Hildebrand, S. (1997, July). Still not equal: Closing the library gender gap. *Library Journal,* pp. 44–46.

Hilo Public Library. (1996). Unpublished library literacy survey. Hilo, HI: Author.

Hook, C., & Rosenshine, B. (1979). Accuracy of teacher reports of their classroom behavior. *Review of Educational Research, 49*(1), 1–12.

Hopey, C. (1998a). Making technology happen in adult education. In C. Hopey (Ed.), *Technology, basic skills, and adult education: Getting ready and moving forward* (pp. 3–9) [ERIC series no. 372]. Columbus, OH: ERIC.

Hopey, C. (Ed.). (1998b). *Technology, basic skills, and adult education: Getting ready and moving forward* [ERIC series no. 372]. Columbus, OH: ERIC.

Horton, M., Kohl, J., & Kohl, H. (1998). *The long haul: An autobiography.* New York: Teachers College Press.

Howard, K. (Ed.). (1998). *The emerging school library media center: Historical issues and perspectives.* Englewood, CO: Libraries Unlimited.

Hueretz, L., Gordon, R., & Gordon, M. (2003). Impact of public access computing on rural and small town libraries. *Rural Libraries.* Retrieved January 21, 2007, from http://data.webjunction.org/wj/documents/885.pdf

Hull, G. A., Mikulecky, L., St. Clair, R., & Kerka, S. (2003). *Multiple literacies: A compilation for adult educators.* Retrieved January 14, 2007, from http://www.tcall.tamu.edu/erica/docs/compilation-literacies.pdf

Humes, B. (1995, April). *Public libraries and community-based education: Making the connection for lifelong learning* [Proceedings of a conference sponsored by the National Institute on Post-Secondary Education, Libraries, and Lifelong Learning]. Washington, DC: Office of Educational Research and Improvement.

Hursh, D. (2006, May). The crisis in urban education: Resisting neo-liberal policies and forging democratic possibilities. *Educational Researcher, 35*(4), 19–25.

Imel, S. (2001). *Learning technologies in adult education. Myths and realities* (No. 17). Retrieved January 21, 2007, from http://www.nicic.org/Library/017688. (ACVE, 20).

Imel, S. (2003). *Informal adult learning and the internet: Trends and issues* (No. 50). Retrieved January 21, 2007, from http://www.calpro-online.org/ERIC/docgen.asp?tbl=tia&ID=173. (ACVE, 20).

Jackson, P. (1968). *Life in classrooms.* New York: Holt, Rinehart & Winston.

Johnson, A. (1938). *The public library: A people's university.* New York: American Association for Education; Chicago: American Library Association.

Kaestle, C. F. (1991). *Literacy in the United States: Readers and reading since 1880.* New Haven, CT: Yale University Press.

Karasoff, P. (1998). Collaborative partnerships: A review of the literature. In J. Jones (Ed.), *Profiles in collaboration: A comprehensive report of the Professional Development Partnership Projects.* Washington, DC: Academy for Educational Development.

Kegan, R., Broderick, M., Drago-Severson, E., Helsing, D., Popp, N., & Portnow, K. (2006). *Toward a new pluralism in ABE classrooms: Teaching to multiple cultures of mind.* Retrieved January 21, 2007, from http://www.ncsall.net/?id=29

Keilman, J. (2005, June 15). Do you speak computer? Hispanics get helpful boost into English-dominated digital world. *Chicago Tribune.* Retrieved January 21, 2007, from http://www.cddnp.org/SpeakComputer.php

Kerka, S. (1997). *Developing collaborative partnerships* (Practice Application Brief). Retrieved January 21, 2007, from http://www.calpro-online.org/eric/docgen.asp?tbl=pab&ID=71. (ACVE, 19).

Kerka, S. (1998). *Continuing education: Market driven or student-centered?* Retrieved January 21, 2007, from http://www.calpro-online.org/eric/docgen.asp?tbl=archive&ID=A026. (ACVE, 19).

Kingery, W. L. (1990, Fall). The White House Conference on library and information services: Thoughts on productivity, literacy and democracy. *Georgia Librarian,* pp. 67–69.

Kirkpatrick, H., & Cuban, L. (1998a). Computers make kids smarter—right? *Technos Quarterly, 19.* Retrieved January 21, 2007, from http://www.ait.net/technos/tq_07/2cuban.php

Kirkpatrick, H., & Cuban, L. (1998b, July/August). Why should we be worried? What the research says about gender differences, access, use, attitudes, and achievement with computers. *Educational Technology,* pp. 56–61.

Kirsch, I., Jungeblatt, L., & Kolstad, A. (1992). *Adult literacy in America: A first look at the results of the national adult literacy survey.* Washington, DC: U.S. Department of Education.

Kniffel, L. (1988). Conference call: Purveyors or prescribers: What should librarians be? *American Libraries, 29*(5), 66.

Kohl, H. (1967). *36 Children.* New York: New American Library.

Kozma, R., & Shank, P. (1998). Connecting with the 21st century: Technology in support of educational reform. In C. Dede (Ed.), *Learning with technology* (pp. 3–30). Alexandria, VA: Association for Supervision and Curriculum Development.

Kretzmann, J., & Rans, S. (2006). *The engaged library: Chicago stories of community-building.* Retrieved January 21, 2007, from http://www.urbanlibraries.org/files/ULC_PFSC_Engaged_0206.pdf

Kronkosky Charitable Foundation. (2005, March). *Public libraries.* Retrieved January 21, 2007, from http://kronkosky.org/search/browse.aspx?q=Research_Briefs

Kulik, J. (1994). Meta-analytic studies of findings on computer-based instruction. In E. Baker & H. O'Neill (Eds.), *Technology assessment in education and training* (pp. 9–33). Hillsdale, NJ: Erlbaum.

Kulik, J. (2003). *Effects of using instructional technology in elementary and secondary schools: What controlled evaluations say.* Retrieved January 21, 2007, from http://www.sri.com/policy/csted/reports/sandt/it/Kulik_ITinK-12_Main_ Report.pdf

Kulik, C., & Kulik, J. (1991). Effectiveness of computer-based instruction: An updated analysis. *Computers in Human Behavior, 7,* 75–94.

Labaree, D. F. (1997). Public goods, private goods: The American struggle over educational goals. *American Educational Research Journal, 34*(1), 39–81.

Lafer, G. (2002). *The job training charade.* Ithaca, NY: Cornell University Press.

Lagemann, E. C. (1989). *Politics of knowledge: Carnegie Corporation.* Middleton, CT: Wesleyan Press.

Lankshear, C., & Knobel, M. (2004). *New literacies: Changing knowledge and classroom learning.* New York: Open University Press.

Lankshear, C., Snyder, I., with Green, B. (2000). *Teachers and techno-literacy: Managing literacy, technology, and learning in schools.* St. Leonards, Australia: Allen & Unwin.

Larson, J. (Ed.). (2001). *Literacy as snake oil.* New York: Peter Lang.

Lauren, P. (Ed.). (1974). *Diplomacy: New approaches in history, theory and policy.* New York: Free Press.

Learned, W. (1924). *The American public library and the diffusion of knowledge.* New York: Harcourt, Brace.

Lee, R. (1966). *Continuing education for adults through the American public library, 1833–1964.* Chicago: American Library Association.

Lenhart, A., Madden, M., & Hitlin, P. (2005, July 27). *Teens and technology: Youth are leading the transition to a fully wired and mobile nation* (Pew Internet and American Life Project report). http://www.pewinternet.org/report_ display .asp?r=162

Lerner, F. (2002). *The story of libraries: From the invention of writing to the computer age.* New York: Continuum International Publishing Group.

Levey, N. (2005, November 29). *L.A. renews its libraries as modern civic centers: More than just housing books, the new and refurbished branches bring people together.* Retrieved January 21, 2007, from http://www.clipi.org/blog/archives/ 220

Levin, H. (1970). *Community control of schools.* Washington, DC: Brookings Institution.

Lewis, L., & Farris, E. (2002). *Program for adults in public library outlets.* Washington, DC: (National Center for Education Statistics report). Retrieved January 14, 2007, from http://nces.ed.gov/pubsearch/pubsinfo.asp?pubid= 2003010

Light, J. (2001). Rethinking the digital divide. *Harvard Educational Review, 71,* 709–733.

Lipschultz, D. (2005). *Making your library literacy-ready.* Chicago: American Library Association.

Lipsman, C. K. (1972). *The disadvantaged and library effectiveness.* Chicago: American Library Association.

Lo, C. (2005, November 30). Got the homework blues? Our libraries have great, free help. *Beacon Hill News: South District Journal,* p. 6.

Lohr, S. (2004, April 22). Libraries wired and reborn. *New York Times,* pp. E1, E4.

Lyman, H. (1954). *Adult education activities in public libraries.* Chicago: American Library Association.

Lyman, H. (1977a). *Literacy and the nation's libraries.* Chicago: American Library Association.

Lyman, H. (1977b). *Reading and the adult new reader.* Chicago: American Library Association.

Main, L., & Whittaker, C. (1991). *Automating literacy: A challenge for libraries.* New York: Greenwood.

Malone, C. (1994, March 27). *Do public libraries matter? A response to Amy A. Begg, Enoch Pratt free library and its services to communities of immigrant residents of Baltimore during the progressive era, 1900–1914.* Paper presented at the H-Urban Seminar on the History of Community Organizing and Community-Based Development.

Marshall, R., &, Tucker, M. (1992). *Thinking for a living: Education and the wealth of nations.* New York: Basic Books.

Martin, R. (2001). *Listening up: Reinventing ourselves as teachers and students.* Portsmouth, NH: Heinemann.

Martin, W. J. (1989). *Community librarianship: Changing the face of public libraries.* London: Bingley.

Mathews, A. J., Chute, A., & Cameron, C. A. (1986). Meeting the literacy challenge: A federal perspective. *Library Trends, 35*(2), 219–241.

Mathews, J. (1988). *Escalante: The best teacher in America.* New York: Henry Holt.

Mayer, D. (1999). Measuring instructional practice: Can policymakers trust survey data? *Educational Evaluation and Policy Analysis, 21*(1), 29–45.

Mayer, R. (Ed.). (2005). *The Cambridge handbook of multimedia learning.* New York: Cambridge University Press.

McClure, C. (1994). Network literacy: A role for libraries? *Information technology and libraries, 13,* 115–125.

McClure, C., Bertot, J. C., & Zweizig, D. L. (1994). *Public libraries and the internet: Study results, policy issues, and recommendations.* Washington, DC: National Commission on Libraries and Information Science.

McDonald, B. (1966). *Literacy activities in public libraries: A report of the study of services to adults.* Chicago: American Library Association.

McKnight, J. (1987). Regenerating community. *Social Policy, 17*(2), 54–58.

Means, B. (1995). *Technology's role in education reform.* Menlo Park, CA: SRI International.

Merriam, S., & Cunningham, P. (Eds.). (1989). *Handbook of adult and continuing education.* San Francisco: Jossey-Bass.

Meyer, J., & Rowan, B. (1977). Institutional organizations: Formal structure as myth and ceremony. *American Journal of Sociology, 83,* 340–363.

Meyer, J. W., & Scott, R. (1983). *Organizational environments: Ritual and rationality.* London: Sage.

Michie, J., & Holton, B. (2005). *Fifty years of supporting children's learning: A history of public school libraries and federal legislation from 1953 to 2000* [NCES 2005-311]. Washington, DC: National Center for Education Statistics.

Molz, P., & Dain, P. (1999). *Civic space/cyberspace: The American public library in the information age.* Cambridge, MA: MIT Press.

Monroe, M. (1963). *Library adult education: Biography of an idea.* New York: Scarecrow Press.

Monroe, M. (1979, Fall). Emerging patterns of community service. *Library Trends,* pp. 129–137.

Monroe, M. (1986, Fall). The evolution of literacy programs in the context of library adult education. *Library Trends,* pp. 197–205.

Mossberger, C., Tolbert, C. J., & Stansbury, M. (2003). *Virtual inequality: Beyond the digital divide.* Washington, DC: Georgetown University Press.

Murnane, R., & Levy, F. (1996). *Teaching the new basic skills.* New York: Free Press.

National Center for Education Statistics. (2005). *Public libraries in the United States: Fiscal year 2003* [NCES 2005-3]. Washington, DC: U.S. Department of Education, Institute of Educational Sciences.

National Commission on Excellence in Education. (1983). *A nation at risk.* Washington, DC: U.S. Government Printing Office.

Nauratil, M. (1985). *Public libraries and non-traditional clienteles: The politics of special services.* Westport, CT: Greenwood Press.

Nixon, S., & Ponder, T. (2001). Literacy and technology: Thinking through the process. In G. A. Decandido (Ed.), *Literacy and libraries: Learning from case studies* (pp. 116–123). Chicago: American Library Association.

Nunberg, G. (1998). Will libraries survive? *American Prospect, 9*(41), 16–23.

O'Connor, S., & Guerra, D. (2001). The Brooklyn Public Library and technology for literacy. In G. A. Decandido (Ed.), *Literacy and libraries: Learning from case studies* (pp. 124–134). Chicago: American Library Association.

Olgren, C. (2000). Learning strategies for learning technologies. In E. J. Burge (Ed.), *The strategic use of learning technologies* (pp. 7–16). San Francisco: Jossey-Bass.

Omnitrak Research and Marketing Group. (1989). *Hawai'i Statewide Literacy Assessment (HSLA).* Honolulu, HI: Author.

1 to 1 learning: A review and analysis by the Metiri Group. (2006). Retrieved January 14, 2007, from images.apple.com/education/k12/onetoone/pdf/1_to_1_white_paper.pdf

O'Neil, J. (2004). Library lessons. *NEA Today.* Retrieved January 14, 2007, from http://www.nea.org/neatoday/0410/library.html

Oppenheimer, T. (1998, October 1). Technology counts. *Education Week,* pp. 7, 8.

Oppenheimer, T. (2003). *The flickering mind.* New York: Random House.

Osborne, R., & Orange, S. (Eds.). (2004). *From outreach to equity: Innovative models of library policy and practice.* Chicago: American Library Association.

Papert, S. (1980). *Mindstorms.* New York: Basic Books.

Parker, A. (1997). *Purifying America: Women, cultural reform, and pro-censorship activism, 1973–1933.* Urbana: University of Illinois Press.

Patterson, J. T. (1986). *America's struggle against poverty, 1900–1985.* Cambridge, MA: Harvard University Press.

Patterson, J. T. (1996). *Grand expectations: The United States, 1945–1974.* New York: Oxford University Press.

Pencils down: Technology's answer to testing. (2003, May 8). *Education Week.* Retrieved January 14, 2007, from http://counts.edweek.org/sreports/tc03/

Phinney, E. (1956). *Library adult education in action: Five case studies.* Chicago: American Library Association.

Pickeral, T. (2002). *Learning that lasts: How service-learning can become an integral part of schools, states, and communities.* Retrieved January 14, 2007, from http://www.clemson.edu/ICSLTE/resources/docs/LearningThatLasts.pdf

Pond, P. (1998). The history of the American Association of School Librarians, 1896–1951. In K. Howard (Ed.), *The emerging school library media center: Historical issues and perspectives* (pp. 207–226). Englewood, CO: Libraries Unlimited.

Porter, K., Cuban, S., & Comings, J. (2005). *One day I will make it: A study of persistence in library literacy programs.* New York: MDRC. Retrieved January 21, 2007, from http://www.mdrc.org/project_publications_32_22.html

Powell, W. W., & Dimaggio, P. J. (1991). *The new institutionalism in organizational analysis.* Chicago: University of Chicago Press.

President's Committee of Advisors on Science and Technology, Panel on Educational Technology. (1997, March). *Report to the President on the use of technology to strengthen K–12 education in the United States.* Washington, DC: Executive Office of the President.

Pritchard, S. (1994, June). Backlash, backwater or back to the drawing board. *Wilson Library Bulletin,* pp. 42–46.

Puacz, J. (2005). Libraries + nonprofits: Add up to profitable community partnerships. *Computers in Libraries, 25*(2), 13–15.

Public libraries as partners in youth development. (1999). New York: DeWitt-Wallace Readers Digest Fund.

Public Policy Institute of New York State. (2003, April 20). *A laptop for every student?* Retrieved January 21, 2007, from http://www.ppinys.org/reports/2003/laptops.pdf

Putnam, R., & Feldstein, L. (2003). *Better together: Restoring the American community.* New York: Simon & Schuster.

Quezada, S. (1992). Strengthening the library network for literacy. *Wilson Library Bulletin, 64*(6), 26–31.

Rachal, J. R. (1990). *The American library adult education movement: The diffusion of knowledge and the democratic ideal, 1924–1933.* Retrieved January 21, 2007, from http://www.distance.syr.edu/rachal.html

Radford, G. (1998). Flaubert, Foucault, and the bibliotheque fantastique: Toward a postmodern epistemology for library science. *Library Trends, 46*(4).

Radway, J. (1994). Beyond Mary Bailey and old maid librarians. *Journal of Education for Library and Information Science, 35*(4), 275–295.

Ranganathan, S. R. (1963). *The five laws of library science.* Bombay, India: Asia Publishing House.

Ravitch, D. (1983). *The troubled crusade.* New York: Basic Books.

Reich, R. (1991). *The work of nations.* New York: Knopf.

Reid, C. (1997). Down and outsourced in Hawai'i. *American Libraries, 28*(6), 56–57.

Resnick, L. B., & Glennan, T. K., Jr. (2002). Leadership for learning: A theory of action for urban school districts. In A. M. Hightower, M. S. Knapp, J. A. Marsh, & M. W. McLaughlin (Eds.), *School districts and instructional renewal* (pp. 160–172). New York: Teachers College Press.

Retooling literacy for the 21st century [Special issue]. (1998). *American Libraries*, 29(11).

Riley, R. (1996). *Putting the pieces together: Comprehensive school-linked strategies for children and families*. Washington, DC: U.S. Department of Education.

Rockman, S. (2003, Fall). Learning from laptops. *Threshold*. Retrieved January 21, 2007, from http://www.b-g.k12.ky.us/Tech/Laptops.pdf

Rogers, E. (1995). *Diffusion of innovations*. New York: The Free Press.

Rolstad, G. (1990). Literacy services in public libraries. In K. Heim & D. Wallace (Eds.), *Adult services: An enduring focus for public libraries* (pp. 245–263). Chicago: American Library Association.

Rose, E. (1917). *Bridging the gulf: Work with Russian Jews and other newcomers, Seward Park Branch New York Public Library*. New York: Immigrant Publication Society.

Rosen, D. (2000). Using electronic technology in adult literacy education. In J. Comings, B. Garner, & C. Smith (Eds.), *The Annual Review of Adult Learning and Literacy, 1*. San Francisco: Jossey-Bass.

Rosenbaum, M., Altman, D., & Blendon, R. (2000, February 29). *Survey shows widespread enthusiasm for high technology*. Retrieved January 14, 2007, from http://www.npr.org/programs/specials/poll/technology/

Rosenfeld, G. (1971). *Shut those thick lips*. New York: Holt Rinehart.

Ross-Gordon, J. M., Martin, L., & Briscoe, D. (Eds.). (1990). *New directions for adult and continuing education, No. 48: Serving culturally diverse populations*. San Francisco: Jossey-Bass.

Roszak, T. (1994). *The cult of information: A neo-Luddite treatise on high-tech, artificial intelligence, and the true art of thinking*. Berkeley: University of California Press.

Roush, W. (2005). The infinite library. *Technology Review*. Retrieved January 14, 2007, from http://www.technologyreview.com/Infotech/14408/

Salter, J., & Salter, C. (1991). *Literacy and the library*. Denver, CO: Libraries Unlimited.

Samuelson, R. (2002, March 20). Debunking the digital divide. *Washington Post*, p. A33. Retrieved January 21, 2007, from http://www.washingtonpost.com/ac2/wp-dyn/A53118-2002Mar19?language=printer

Sandholtz, J., & Kelly, B. (2004). Teachers, not technicians: Rethinking technical expectations for teachers. *Teachers College Record*, 106(3), 487–512.

Sandholtz, J., Ringstaff, C., & Dwyer, D. (1997). *Teaching with technology: Creating student centered classrooms*. New York: Teachers College Press.

Schmidt, S. (1978). A history of ABE services in public libraries. *Drexel Library Quarterly*, 4, 5–12

Schramm, W. (1977). *Big media, little media*. Beverly Hills, CA: Sage.

Schuman, P. (Ed.). (1983). *Social responsibilities of librarians*. New York: Bowker.

Scott, A. F. (1991). *Natural allies: Women's associations in American history*. Urbana: University of Illinois Press.

Scott, W. R. (2005). Institutionalization theory: Contributing to a theoretical research program. In K. G. Smith & M. A. Hitt (Eds.), *Great minds in management: The process of theory development* (Ch. 22). Oxford, UK: Oxford University Press. Retrieved January 14, 2007, from http://www.si.umich.edu/ICOS/Institutional%20Theory%20Oxford04.pdf

Shera, J. H. (1965). *Foundations of the public library: The origins of the public library movement in New England, 1629–1855.* Hamden, CT: Shoestring Press.

Shriver, M. (2002). *Case study: What's really involved in public library services to immigrants.* Report, University of Michigan School of Information.

Silvernail, D., & Lane, D. (2004, February). *The impact of Maine's one-to-one laptop program on middle school teachers and students* (Research Report #1). Portland: Maine Education Policy Research Institute, University of Southern Maine. Retrieved January 14, 2007, from http://mainegov-images.informe.org/mlte/articles/research/MLTIPhaseOneEvaluationReport2004.pdf

Simonton, W. (Ed.). (1986). *Advances in librarianship* (Vol. 14). New York: Academic Press.

Skocpol, T., & Sommers, M. (1980, April). The uses of comparative history in macrosocial inquiry. *Comparative Studies in Society and History, 22,* 174–181.

Small, S., & Supple, A. (2001). Communities as systems: Is a community more than the sum of its parts? In A. Booth & A. Crouter (Eds.), *Does it take a village? Community effects on children, adolescents, and families* (pp. 61–70). Mahwah, NJ: Erlbaum.

Smith, E. G. (1984). The literacy education gap: The involvement of public libraries in literacy education. *Library and Information Science Research, 6,* 75–94.

Spangenberg, G. (1996). *Even anchors need lifelines: Public libraries in adult literacy.* New York: Spangenberg Resources and The Center for the Book.

Spielberger, J., Horton, C., & Michaels, L. (2004). *New on the shelf: Summary of key findings from the evaluation of libraries as partners in youth development.* New York: Wallace Foundation.

Spires, T., & Hill, J. B. (n.d.). *Outsourcing and privatization in libraries: Ethical concerns.* Retrieved January 21, 2007, from http://exlibris.memphis.edu/ethics21/archives/05eei/papers/spireshill.pdf

Squire, K., & Stenkeuhler, C. (2005, April). Meet the gamers. *LibraryJournal.com.* Retrieved January 21, 2007, from http://www.libraryjournal.com/article/CA516033.html

State of the Union Address. (2002, January 30). *New York Times,* p. A22.

Stites, R. (1998). Adult learning theory: An argument for technology. In C. Hopey (Ed.), *Technology, basic skills, and adult education* (pp. 51–56) (ERIC series no 372). Columbus, OH: ERIC.

Strand, K. S., Murullo, S., Cutforth, N., Stoecker, R., & Donohue, P. (2003). *Community-based research and higher education: Principles and practices.* San Francisco: Jossey-Bass.

Street, B. (1984). *Literacy in theory and practice.* Cambridge, UK: Cambridge University Press.

Sumerford, S. (2001). Creating a community of readers to fight functional illiteracy. In R. Osborne & C. D. Hayden (Eds.), *Outreach to equity: Innovative models of library policy and practice* (pp. 97–105). Chicago: American Library Association, Office for Literacy and Outreach Services.

Survey shows widespread enthusiasm for high technology. (2000, March 2). Retrieved January 14, 2007, from http://www.npr/programs/specials/poll/technology/index.html

Symons, A., & Stoffle, C. J. (1988). When values conflict. *American Libraries, 29*(5), 56–58.

Talan, C. (1990). Family literacy makes ene. *Bottom Line, 3*(4), 46–51.

Technology counts (Student perspective section). (1999, September 23). *Education Week.*

Technology counts. (2002, May 9). *Education Week,* p. 54.

Thurow, L. (1992). *Head to head: The coming economic battle among Japan, Europe, and America.* New York: Morrow.

Tight, M. (2004). *Key concepts in adult education and training.* London: Routledge.

To read, to write, to understand. (1997, May). *American Libraries, 28*(5).

Toch, T. (1991). *In the name of excellence.* New York: Oxford University Press.

Trotter, A., et al. (1997, November 10). Technology counts: Schools and reform in the information age. *Education Week* (Suppl.). Retrieved January 14, 2007, from http://www.edweek.org/sreports/tc/

Trotter, A. (2003, March 26). Study shows a thinner "digital divide." *Education Week,* p. 9.

21st century literacy. (1998). *American Libraries, 29*(11), 1–8.

Tyack, D. (1974). *One best system.* Cambridge, MA: Harvard University Press.

Tyack, D., & Cuban, L. (1995). *Tinkering toward utopia.* Cambridge, MA: Harvard University Press.

Tyack, D., & Hansot, E. (1982). *Managers of virtue.* New York: Basic Books.

Tyack, D., Hansot, E., & Lowe, R. (1984). *Public schools in hard times.* Cambridge, MA: Harvard University Press.

U.S. Department of Education. (n.d.). 21st century community learning centers. Retrieved January 21, 2007, from http://www.ed.gov/programs/21stcclc/index.html

U.S. Department of Education. (1999, Summer). *Technology in after-school programs.* Retrieved January 21, 2007, from http://www.ed.gov/pubs/After_School_Programs/Technology_Programs.html

Van Fleet, C., & Raber, D. (1990). The public library as a social/cultural institution: Alternative perspectives and changing context. In K. Heim & D. Wallace (Eds.), *Adult services: An enduring focus for public libraries* (pp. 456–500). Chicago: American Library Association.

Van House, N., Lynch, M. J., McClure, C. R., Zweizig, D. L., & Rodger, E. J. (1987). *Output measures for public libraries: A manual of standardized procedures.* Chicago: American Library Association, Public Library Association.

Vann, S. (Ed.). (1978). *Melvil Dewey: His enduring presence in librarianship.* Littleton, CO: Libraries Unlimited.

Van Slyck, A. (1995). *Free to all: Carnegie libraries and American culture, 1890–1920.* Chicago: University of Chicago Press.

Viadero, D. (2005, November 16). Teacher logs reveal how class time is really spent. *Education Week,* p. 7.

Walter, V., Mediavilla, C., Braun, L., & Meyers, E. (2005). *Learning in libraries: White paper on principles and practices to public libraries for children and young adults during out-of-school-time.* Retrieved January 21, 2007, from www.urbanlibraries.org/files/LiLreport.pdf

Ward, A., & Watson-Ellam, L. (2005). Reading beyond school: Literacies in a neighborhood library. *Canadian Journal of Education*. Retrieved January 21, 2007, from www.csse.ca/CJE/Articles/FullText/CJE28-1-2/CJE28-1-2-ward.pdf

Warschauer, M. (2003). *Technology and social inclusion: Rethinking the digital divide*. Cambridge, MA: MIT Press.

Weigand, D. (1986, Fall). The library-learner dynamic in a changing world. *Library Trends*, pp. 187–192.

Whiteside, C. (2004). Central Valley digital network: Partners in bridging the digital divide. In R. Osborne & S. Orange (Eds.), *From outreach to equity: Innovative models of library policy and practice* (pp. 53–55). Chicago: American Library Association.

Wiebe, R. (1967). *The search for order, 1877–1920*. New York: Hill and Wang.

Wiegand, W. (1998, January). The politics of cultural authority. *American Libraries*, pp. 80–82.

Wiegand, W. (1994). Tunnel vision and blind spots: What the past tells us about the present: Reflections on the twentieth century history of American librarianship. *Library Quarterly*, 69(1), 1–32.

Wiegand, W. W., & Davis, D. (Eds.). (1994). *Encyclopedia of library history*. New York: Garland.

Williams, S. M., Burgess, K., Bray, K., Bransford, J. D., Goldman, S., & Cognition and Technology Group at Vanderbilt. (1998). Technology and learning in schools for thought classrooms. In C. Dede (Ed.), *The 1998 Yearbook for the Association for Supervision and Curriculum Development: Learning with technology* (pp. 97–120). Alexandria, VA: Association for Supervision and Curriculum Development.

Witherell, C., & Noddings, N. (1990). *Stories lives tell: Narratives and dialogue in education*. New York: Teachers College Press.

Wonacott, M. (2001). *Technology literacy*. Retrieved January 14, 2007, from http://www.calpro-online.org/eric/docgen.asp?tbl=digests&ID=118.

Yohalem, N., & Pittman, K. (2003). *Public libraries as partners in youth development: Lessons and voices from the field*. Washington, DC: Forum for Youth Investment and Dewitt-Wallace Readers Digest Fund.

Youth in ABE [Special issue]. (2004, June). *Focus on basics*, 7(A). Retrieved January 14, 2007, from http://www.ncsall.net/?id=123

Zweizig, D., Robbins, J., & Johnson, D. (1988). *Libraries and literacy education: Comprehensive survey report*. Washington, DC: U.S. Department of Education.

About the Authors

Photo by Janice Cuban

Sondra Cuban is a lecturer in Educational Research and a researcher with the Lancaster Literacy Research Centre, Lancaster University, England. She graduated from Sonoma State University with a B.A. from the Hutchins School of Interdisciplinary Studies, got an M.L.I.S. in Library & Information Science at the University of Hawai'i–Manoa, and served as a public librarian in Hawai'i. She has a Ph.D. from the University of Wisconsin–Madison and was a research associate for 4 years at Harvard's National Center for the Study of Adult Learning and Literacy before serving as assistant professor in Adult Education at Seattle University. Her research focuses on adult literacy and community technologies, participation and engagement of adult learners, health literacy, workplace literacy, and women and literacy. Her book *Serving New Immigrant Communities in the Libraries* (2007) focuses on these issues.

Larry Cuban is professor emeritus of Education at Stanford University. He has taught courses in the history of school reform, curriculum, instruction, and leadership. He has been a faculty sponsor of the Stanford/Schools Collaborative and Stanford's Teacher Education Program. His background in the field of education prior to becoming a professor included 14 years of teaching high school social studies in ghetto schools, directing a teacher education program that prepared returning Peace Corps volunteers to teach in inner-city schools, and serving 7 years as a district superintendent. Trained as a historian, he received a B.A. degree from the University of Pittsburgh in 1955 and an M.A. from Cleveland's Case-Western Reserve University 3 years later. On completing his Ph.D. work at Stanford University in 1974, he assumed the superintendency of the Arlington, Virginia, public schools, a position he held until returning to Stanford in 1981. Since 1988, he has taught three times in local high school semester-long courses in U.S. history and economics. Between 1981 and 2001, students in the School of Education selected Cuban for an award in excellence in teaching seven times.

His major research interests focus on the history of curriculum and instruction, educational leadership, school reform, and the uses of technology in classrooms. His most recent books are *Cutting Through the Hype: A Taxpayer's Guide to School Reform* (2006, with Jane David), *The Blackboard and the Bottom Line: Why Schools Can't Be Businesses* (2004), *Powerful Reforms with Shallow Roots: Improving Urban Schools* (2003, edited with Michael Usdan), *Why Is It So Hard To Get Good Schools?* (2003), and *Oversold and Underused: Computers in the Classroom* (2001).

Index